THE ZEN WINEMAKER

D1467226

The Zen Winemaker

Follow Your Dreams
Overcome Your Fears

Darius Miller

Copyright © 2020 Darius F. Miller All rights reserved

The characters and events portrayed in this book are fictitious. Any similarity to real persons, living or dead, is coincidental and not intended by the author.

No part of this book may be reproduced, or stored in a retrieval system, or transmitted in any form or by any means, electronic, mechanical, photocopying, recording, or otherwise, without express written permission of the publisher.

Printed in the United States of America

*To my wife Lisa who has been my soulmate,
my partner and my friend for so many years.*

"If you say that getting the money is the most important thing, you'll spend your life completely wasting your time. You'll be doing things you don't like doing in order to go on living, that is to go on doing things you don't like doing, which is stupid."

~~ Alan Watts ~~

FOREWORD

Everything in this book is true – except for the fictional parts. Though some of the characters and situations have been changed, I hope the message remains clear and memorable. I am humbled and honored to share my life and the lives of others within this text and share the lessons we have learned. This wisdom is ageless and universal, relying not on deep complex understandings, but normal every-day observances and actions.

Who knew that a simple grape could shed light on age-old questions such as: who am I, and what is my purpose? These questions are often asked, though rarely answered. And if answered, are rarely followed, which is a shame, but understandable.

It took me two major life events to finally 'wake up' and to start following a passion opposed to a paycheck. When you realize in your core that waking up is a blessing and not a given, your priorities change. Stress and poor choices were killing me as I chased that almighty dollar. I realized something had to change. I walked away from a lucrative tech job and followed a dream to open a winery along with my wife – we wanted to create a place where people could 'Uncork, Sip back and Relax' and this is what we have done.

This is the story of Joe, who learns 5 simple techniques from a winemaker that allow him to find his purpose and follow his dreams while helping others along the way. There are pieces of Joe in me, and I suspect in you. I hope this simple book will help you fulfill your dreams during this short journey called life.

If you are ever in San Diego, look up Koi Zen Cellars and come on by. We would love to meet you and show you around.

Cheers,
Darius Miller
The Zen Winemaker

PROLOGUE

Thump! The steering wheel shook and Joe's hand began to throb. A scowl and clenched jaw reflected at him in the rearview mirror. One more damn trip, he thought. The engine roared into life and for the third time this morning, he was heading to Home Depot – all because he forgot a twenty-five-cent washer. White-knuckled and filled with frustration, he shifted into drive and accelerated rapidly.

The day had started off crappy – literally. Lucy, who was three years old, had tried to stuff purple monkey down the toilet and then proceeded to do her business on top of it. Being a good girl, she dutifully flushed, overflowing the bowl with messy water and, yes, crap. It was everywhere: the floor, walls and the ceiling – how that happened no one could explain, but there it was on the ceiling.

Not a good way to start a Saturday, especially after the rough few weeks of constant client calls, long boring meetings, the merging of two companies in a hostile takeover and the threat of Joe's branch closing. All Joe wanted to do was to sleep in – just once, just for a few extra minutes – but no. Armed with a bad attitude, crappy clothes, and wet feet, he fumed towards the hardware store once more.

The San Diego morning gloom was giving way to blue skies and streaks of light reflected off the glass commercial buildings lining World Trade Drive. Rounding the bend, there it was, a message from the heavens: 'Wine Tasting' flapped on a purple flag. Without thinking, Joe turned the wheel hard into a nondescript business park. The parking lot was empty except for one car parked beside a second purple flag that read 'Open.'

1

The sign above the door of suite P read 'Koi Zen Cellars Craft Winery.'

Stepping out of the car, Joe looked around at all the suites in the small business park, each the same as their neighbor. On each door was a capital letter and above was a sign with the company name. The façades were simple concrete, smoked glass doors, and windows. There were no grapes, no vines, and this did not look anything like any winery Joe had ever visited. Wineries were always out in the country along some dangerous windy road. But this was different – very different. Maybe because of the dread of his chores, or because the simple stylized winery sign piqued his curiosity, but doing a little wine tasting at 11:45 in the morning seemed a much better option than dealing with all the crap in his life now.

With trepidation, he pulled open the glass door. A wave of rich aromatic cold air washed over him as he stepped into a magical place.

CHAPTER 1

"Hello. Welcome to Koi Zen Cellars," a deep soothing friendly voice beckoned from across the dimly lit room.

Joe had been in thousands of business parks, visiting clients and selling his insurance policies, but this was like nothing he had ever seen before. Gone were the typical white walls, white drop ceiling tiles, fluorescent light, and cheap indoor-outdoor carpets. What stood before him was something new, something welcoming and something exciting. He stumbled over the gap between expectations and reality. The jolt froze him for a moment, and he stood in the threshold waiting for his eyes to adjust to the dim lights, dark colors, and hardwood floors.

"Not what you expected?"

"Uh, no... I mean, um, no, not really."

"Well, come on in, you're letting the fruit flies in."

"Fruit flies?"

"Yeah, those pesky little critters that show up during harvest, along with the crickets and praying mantises."

"The crickets and the what?"

"Crickets and praying mantises bring us good luck! We welcome them every year during harvest. We need as much luck as possible, and we take and appreciate every blessing that nature gives us. We just received 20,000 pounds of Syrah and it has just begun to ferment. The fresh fruit and fermentation attract fruit flies. The fruit flies attract the crickets, and the crickets attract the praying mantises. And the wine attracted you," he chuckled.

The door closed slowly behind Joe. Three hours ago, he was up to his armpits in a broken toilet, crap, a soaking wet purple monkey, and two trips to Home Depot. Now he found himself standing inside of a business park office suite, which was not a suite but a winery, talking about crickets. He shook his head in disbelief. Oh, Joe, you need a break, you're losing it, he thought to himself.

Within three steps into the winery, a calming feeling rushed over him. The stress of the morning magically melted away. He was walking into a new world, a new belief, and a new path. But he would realize this only weeks later.

His shoes clicked on the hardwood floors. Drop pendant lights illuminated the soft, rich, dark colors of the walls, each of which was painted a different calming color: mustard, burgundy, spice brown, and sage green. The black granite bar top reflected the drop lights suspended above and the rich dark oak bar drew him closer. Around the room were soft chairs, couches, and tables. The room looked more like a designer home than an office suite – like a great place to hang out and unwind after a tough day. Neatly arranged wine bottles lined the shelves behind the granite bar. Crystal glasses hung upside down, catching glints of light. Sound of running water filled the dim space and a wonderful aroma was thick in the cold air. A slight chill ran over his body as he stood there in amazement, absorbing the details.

He recalled his office: its white walls, cheap paintings, glaring lights, laminate office furniture and opposing cubical enclosures, each cube exactly like the next, all lifeless, each lacking a sense of emotion. A vast yearning swelled in his heart.

The far end of the bar was cluttered with test tubes, a plate full of grapes, papers, beakers, and measuring instruments.

A man with graying hair in a ponytail said with a smile, "Sorry for the mess, but this is a fantastic time to show up."

"How so?"

"We have just started our crush, and this is the first batch of must we are inoculating."

The confusion was apparent on Joe's face.

4

"Sorry, I'm the winemaker, and co-owner of the winery," he said, extending a hand. "And that's my wife Lisa over there – she is the big boss," he said pointing across the room. She smiled and waved.

"Hi, I'm Joe. What exactly are you doing?"

"I am performing a little magic. With the help of Mother Nature, I'm converting these grapes into liquid heaven."

Chuckling, Joe pointed to the plate of grapes and said, "It doesn't seem like it will make a lot of wine."

"True, but follow me, Grasshopper."

Deeper still into the winery was another door that led to the first production area. Ten large plastic vats lined the wall, each chest high, and four-foot square. Each was filled with masses of dark purple grapes.

Gesturing to the room, he said, "This is 20,000 pounds of grapes. What do you think now Joe?"

Sheepishly Joe replied, "I guess first impressions can be wrong."

"So true. You just didn't see the whole picture, that's all. Just a little too quick in wit and tongue."

Joe wasn't sure whether to take that as a compliment or a criticism.

The Winemaker walked over to one of the vats and said, "This bin holds 2000 pounds of grapes. At this point, we have already removed the stems and have gotten the 'must' ready for fermentation. Must is the word used to describe the grape solids, the juice, the skins, and the seeds that are fermented together to produce red wine. Later today, I will 'inoculate' the must, which means to add yeast. The yeast will convert the sugars into alcohol and produce wine."

"I thought wine came from the grocery store," Joe joked.

"I did too when I first started learning about wine over thirty years ago, but now I know better." Both chuckled and wandered back to the tasting room.

"So, what brings you in today Joe?"

Suddenly, Joe's shoulders sagged, and his head dropped down as if a huge weight had been placed upon him. "This morning my daughter Lucy clogged up the toilet, which I broke in my frustration while trying to fix it, and now I am on my third trip to Home Depot and covered in crap."

"I was wondering what that off-aroma was – smells like Brett."

Not knowing what that meant, Joe glanced up sheepishly and said, "Guilty as charged. Not only are my clothes covered in crap, so is my sorry life. I just can't seem to catch a break these days." A look of defeat covered his face.

"Well, maybe a little wine and some good conversation can help. I believe that wine people are good people. They come here to 'uncork, sip back and relax.' So, why do you feel that way?"

Joe started with the story of Lucy, then his job, then his house, then his family – each story becoming more melancholy and depressing.

Eventually, the Winemaker held up his hand, signaling that he'd heard enough. "Let's start with some water to flush out the bad taste in your mouth and in your mind before we taste some fine wine together." He retrieved two glasses and a jug, and began filling Joe's. "If you aren't happy, why don't you just change your life?"

"I can't. My wife Mary is pregnant with our second child. We just bought a house that was over our budget, and I need my job to pay the mortgage. Lucy has some special needs; we have so many bills and…"

The Winemaker continued pouring water into Joe's water glass until it was overflowing onto the bar, maintaining eye contact all the time.

"Hey, you're spilling all over the place."

"So are you." He paused. "Joe, your mind is just like this cup of water. You are so full of why you can't do something, nothing else can get in. You are so full of excuses that you don't even have the capability of accepting the idea of change. The only way to improve your life is to first empty your cup."

"And how do I do that?"

"One drop at a time," he said with a twinkle in his eye. "Want to learn?"

Darius Miller

CHAPTER 2

At 5:30, Joe's alarm clock blared. But he wasn't in bed. Mary reached across the cold sheets and hit the snooze button, quieting the obnoxious noise. She groggily grabbed her bathrobe and stumbled around the house looking for Joe. She found him sitting in the dining room staring at a blank wall.

"Joe, what are you doing sitting here in the dark at 5:30 in the morning?"

Extending five fingers he mouthed, "Five more minutes."

Mary stumbled away towards the bathroom. Sometime later, a cloud of steam emerged ahead of her as she opened the door, hair soaking wet with a towel wrapped around her. Joe was smiling and cooking breakfast.

"Well isn't this a surprise? Why are you in such good spirits? And why were you staring at the wall this morning?"

"I was emptying my cup," he said proudly.

"Emptying your cup?"

"That's right. I'll tell you about it over breakfast. Let me get Lucy up and we can eat breakfast as a family – for once. Right now, I feel life's moving so fast and that I'm going to blink and Lucy will be going off to college."

Over eggs, bacon and hash browns, Joe began to describe meeting the Zen Winemaker and how he needed to empty his mind to allow space for new ideas. "Last night, after you went to bed, I got on the internet and was reading about mindful meditation. With just a few minutes a day, you can change your life around. So, this morning I got up early and tried meditating. You wouldn't believe how many random thoughts bounced around in my head. No wonder I'm so stressed out and always tired."

"How do you meditate?" Mary asked.

"Well, you just sit there and breathe normally with your eyes closed. You simply count each breath, up to ten, then start over. But if you find that your mind has drifted, you start over again at one. I only got to two twice in ten minutes. Every few seconds a new thought popped into my head. There is so much chatter that's going on. I was worried about the restructurings of my division, my upcoming evaluation, paying the bills, random thoughts about what to make for breakfast. I felt like a whole choir of monkeys were chatting away in my head. It was so loud – almost deafening.

"My mind would bounce from subject to subject and it then became a little depressing. I started thinking about the restructurings, and suddenly I'm thinking that I'm not good enough and that Bill is going to get a new position and not me. And how I might get fired because deep down I feel like I'm a bad person and that I don't have any skills. I got scared thinking about losing my job and not being able to pay our bills. It got really depressing."

"Oh honey, you are none of those things. You are a wonderful loving father and you treat me well. You shouldn't get down on yourself – we are just going through some major adjustments right now. With the uncertainty of your job and me being laid off, there is a lot of stress in the house. We will get through this together. But - how is this meditation thing supposed to help you if it makes you feel horrible?"

"I don't know, but all of that bad self-talk in my head can't be good. I know I have to change. I don't know how yet, but at least I'm trying!" he said triumphantly.

Joe jumped into his car full of energy, pep, and a new positive attitude. It lasted for three blocks - until a random car cut him off and his mood slid downhill from there. With the greatest of ease, he slipped back into his 'Poor old Joe, woe is me' mode. He sat moping at this his desk all morning, futzing with this and that, not inspired or effective. He looked at the clock for the hundredth time: the seconds dragged on for minutes and the hours felt like years. With every tick, Joe slipped deeper and deeper into a paralyzing depression of self-pity.

Lunch was a cold ham and cheese sandwich and a side of dried-out carrot sticks. He sat alone at his desk, frustrated and in a bad mood. The afternoon was even worse, with meetings and conflict with his boss. He knew his attitude didn't help, but he just didn't care.

At 4:00 his phone beeped. It was a message from the Winemaker: "Crushing five tons tonight at 6:00." He had no idea what this meant, but he knew he was going to be there. Within an hour he had cranked through his tasks for the day and tidied his desk. He bolted to the door at 5:00:01. On the way home, he called Mary, and simply told her he was going to be home late and to kiss Lucy goodnight – and that he loved her.

It was Monday night and Koi Zen Cellars was closed to the public, but the lights were on and people were milling around inside. Nervous, but excited, Joe entered the winery. He was immediately surrounded by people all wearing similar tee-shirts. There were white shirts, black shirts, green shirts, and burgundy shirts, and all read "Koi Zen Cellars Crush Crew," with an indicator of the vintage – 2016, 2017, 2018, or 2019. Smiling happy faces greeted Joe and welcomed him to "The Crew." Immediately he felt that he belonged and was part of something bigger than his simple life.

The Zen Winemaker came around the corner smiling and said, "Joe, so glad you came tonight. We have 10,000 pounds, which is 5 tons, of fruit to process tonight and we need every hand we can get. Grab a tee-shirt and we will start in just a few minutes – the delivery truck is just a few miles down the road."

He addressed the gathering, and excited faces turned to him. "Okay crew, you know the drill. We will be hand-sorting the fruit, pulling out the MOG and destemming. The fruit will be fermented in four of the forty-eights over there," he said, pointing to the large plastic bins Joe had seen before.

The crew scrambled, towing Joe along, explaining how to sanitize his hands, tools, and buckets, and how the whole process worked. The truck rumbled in and the horn blasted. The weary-eyed driver waved from the window. He had been up all night for the pick and had then driven 500 miles down from Sonoma with the Pinot Noir grapes.

Without any direction from the Winemaker, the crew mobilized. Forklifts pulled the fruit from the truck and staged it, and moved the thousand-pound bins around with grace and precision. Then they got to work destemming. Joe was amazed: not just at the efficiency and dedication each person put into the laborious task of destemming the grapes, but the joy too – everyone was laughing and joking. Bucket by bucket the fruit was hand-sorted, discarding the leaves, stems, and inferior grapes. Joe learned that this was the MOG (material other than grapes). For fermentation, only the best grapes were used in fine wine production. Each bucket was passed to another person standing on a bench, who dropped the grape clusters into the de-stemmer. As the grapes fell into the hopper of the de-stemmer, an auger beneath would slowly grab the clusters and push them into a long rotating cage with holes in it. Inside the cage was a bar with many arms protruding from it. This would move the fruit through the cage, and each whole, well-formed grape would fall into a receiving bin placed under the machine. Other crew members were meticulously picking out small bits of leaves and an occasional stem as the fruit fell from the machine. The only thing left were shiny grapes the size of blackberries.

The Winemaker stood aside overseeing the operations, taking measurements and notes and making small adjustments. The Assistant Winemaker was carefully adding precise amounts of various powders and liquids to assist in fermentation. Music was blaring, people were laughing. The crew efficiently processed the grape clusters bucket by bucket without any direction or control.

When the last bucket dumped into the de-stemmer, the crew cheered and immediately started cleaning up. They cleaned the outside and edges of each bin, then covered the top in plastic, and moved the 2500-pound bin up to the fermentation room. Next, the crew scrubbed all the equipment until it was spotless, mopped, swept and dried the floors, and took all the trash to the dumpster. Joe marveled at the dedication and efficiency of the whole operation, wishing his office worked like this: efficient, fun and with a strong sense of pride. In his office, there was a sense of hostility from the managers and contempt from the staff. The whole place felt dysfunctional.

With everything cleaned up, the crew was exhausted but excited. Each person had a smile, and then the customary round of wine and beer was served. People chatted, told stories, hugged, shared food and had a great time.

Joe sat off to one side, not knowing anyone. The Winemaker came and sat down with him, drinking a beer.

"Joe, what do you think about destemming fruit?"

"It was a lot of hard work and the people were great. You must pay them a whole lot to work so hard."

"I don't pay the Crush Crew. They are all students who want to learn how to make premium wine – this is a class. They understand that the more hands-on experience they get, the better they will be as winemakers in the future. They come, I

13

teach and we all learn together. Even though wine has been made for thousands of years, it is still a great mystery. With every batch we make, we take careful notes of what we did and why we did it. Years later, we see if we were right or not. It's a long process, but a very satisfying one."

"But everyone worked so hard."

"Yes, but they also played hard. When you do something that you truly enjoy or believe in, or something bigger than yourself, it never feels like work. It feels like" – he paused, looking for the words – "like you are giving back to the universe and making it a better place."

"I wish my work felt that way."

"One day it will Grasshopper. You just need to learn more."

It was 11:00 when Joe slipped into bed and kissed Mary on the forehead. She mumbled something and fell fast asleep again. He was tired, sore, sticky and smelled sweet, but for the first time in a long time, he was satisfied – even happy. Reaching over, Joe set his alarm for half an hour early – he wanted time to meditate.

Drifting off to sleep, he wondered at the stark difference between his peers at work and the Crush Crew. One group was uninspired and the other inspirational. No matter what, he wanted to be part of the Crush Crew – to do something bigger than himself, something that would bring joy to others regardless of how hard he had to work to get there. Within a few moments, he had drifted off into a deep relaxing sleep filled with dreams of new possibilities and interesting paths to walk.

CHAPTER 3

Grabbing his paper lunch bag, Joe headed towards the break room. The morning had been uninspiring and frustrating. His boss was criticizing his lack of sales, but Joe didn't care: he was disengaged and frustrated with his life. He sat down heavily at a table with four of his work friends.

"Why the long face Joe? Ham sandwich again?" Bob asked. Everyone else giggled.

"No, it's not that. It's... it's this place. I'm in the wrong terroir."

Confused, Sally asked, "The wrong what?"

"Terroir. It's a French word. I think it means 'place' or something like that. Over the weekend I stopped at this winery over in Rancho Bernardo and started talking to the Winemaker. He explained it to me. He said that there are over 8,000 different types of wine grapes, and each thrives best in a very specific climate. Some varietals – that's what you call types of grapes – like cold foggy mornings and hot afternoons. Some like high elevation and wind. Some like granite, or shale, or clay soils. Some like hot days and cold nights, and some like temperate weather. Some like lots of water and others like it bone-dry.

"The whole thing is very complicated, but the bottom line is that if you plant a grape in the wrong place, it won't grow well. The Winemaker said, 'If you start with good grapes you have a fighting chance of making a decent bottle of wine, otherwise you have drain cleaner.'"

Everyone chuckled.

"I've had some pretty bad wines," said George.

Clark responded, "Yeah, not as bad as the one I had last night! It cost me a whole three dollars."

"Most days, I feel like drain cleaner; something that no one cares about. I am planted in the wrong place. It's depressing and stifling, and I don't like what I'm doing here. I am constantly frustrated, or nervous about the restructure or losing my job, but I don't know what to do about it."

Everyone sat silently for a few moments. The tension was broken when Sally asked, "Then what do you want to do Joe?"

"I don't know Sally. I wish I did, but this isn't it. What about you? What's your ideal job, what is your terroir?"

"I always wanted to be a doctor. I wanted to find a cure for or cancer. My dad died of prostate cancer when I was thirteen, and I always wanted to help people. What about you Frank?"

"I wanted to be an architect and design great buildings like museums or cathedrals, but I just kind of fell into this job and got stuck here."

"I want to be a yoga teacher," said George. He was six foot three and looked like a giant teddy bear.

Clark was the last to respond. In hushed dejection, he stated, "I don't care, as long as it pays the bills."

Everyone looked at him, wondering how he could have said such a thing. But then they all realized they were doing exactly that. Not one of them was following their dreams. They were all sitting at the same lunch table, working in the same department at the same company, as they had been for the last 5 years.

"So, we have an 'I don't care,' a yoga instructor, an architect, a doctor and an 'I don't know,'" said Sally glancing at Joe. "And yet we are all working as life insurance reps. What's wrong with this picture?"

Everyone sat shaking their heads. Something was wrong but no one knew what to do.

Trying to lighten the mood, Clark said, "Come on guys, this place isn't so bad. It pays the bills, and the work is okay – sort of. Why would you want to risk a sure thing?"

"Clark," Sally said, "this place isn't a sure thing if you think about it. We are going through a restructuring, and no one knows how that is going to change our lives. We don't even know if we are going to be here after the changes. Heck, we don't even know if we are going to wake up in the morning."

"Sally, don't be such a downer. All we can do is hope and pray that things will work out," Clark chimed in.

"That's not a good plan Clark. I don't want to be blindsided by something out of my control. Let me tell you, I'm going to be in control!"

"So, what are you going to do Sally?"

After a long pause, with her head hung low, she responded, "I don't know."

###

Joe spent the rest of the afternoon doodling on a scratch pad next to his computer thinking about what Sally had said and trying to figure out where to find his terroir.

He left at 4:32. At that moment, he just didn't care what his boss thought.

Darius Miller

CHAPTER 4

That night's dinner wasn't exactly a thrilling event. Joe's head hung low, and he was pushing his food back and forth across the plate.

Eventually, Mary couldn't take it anymore. "Joe, sweetheart, what's the matter?"

"I'm all mixed up inside. I hate my job, but I can't leave. It pays the bills, and with a new baby on the way and the house mortgage..."

"Joe, stop! I want you to be happy! We can figure this out."

"But, the bills and the..."

She shushed him with one finger. Lovingly she said, "Joe, it sounds like you need to go empty your cup again."

As if by magic, Joe's phone binged. The message read "Punchdown 2:00 AM!" A smile spread across Joe's face. "Honey, I have a mission."

9:14, 10:21, 11:32, 12:03, 1:11: Joe kept glancing at the blue glow of the clock on the nightstand table, unable to sleep, excited and unsure. He swung his feet out of bed and threw on a pair of sweats. The crisp October air blasted his left ear from the open car window, Punchdown? What's a punchdown? he wondered.

The parking lot was empty save for a lone car parked in front of Koi Zen Cellars. The aromas of fermentation were overpowering as he entered the winery. Rich smells of bready yeast, fruit, jam and some other kind of magical elixir were in the air. He followed the light towards the production area.

"Hi Joe, glad to see you. Thanks for coming by."

"Tonight, we have to punch down each of these ten bins. You see, fermentation is a natural process. Do you see that white film on the grapes? That's yeast. Yeast is everywhere but likes to do two things. Want to know what?"

Intrigued, Joe replied, "Yeah?"

"They want to eat and to multiply. Yeast consumes sugars and turns them into alcohol. It's their waste product – their pee, to put it crudely. And it is toxic to them. But they keep eating sugar, turning it into alcohol and multiplying faster than rabbits. Over ten days this yeast colony will grow from a few to billions. Once all the sugar is consumed, we have dry wine.

"During this process, three things happen. First, sugar is metabolized by the yeast. This creates alcohol, heat and carbon dioxide. The carbon dioxide causes the grape skins to float to the top, creating what we call a 'cap.' This cap can get over two feet thick, and traps the heat below. This causes three problems. First, yeast doesn't like to be hot. They produce all kinds of bad aromas and flavors - and just get downright nasty if they get too hot. If it gets too hot, around ninety degrees Fahrenheit, there is a good chance they will go into hibernation. If they do that, they don't want to wake up, and it is a real challenge restarting a stuck fermentation.

"Second, the yeast wants to breathe. Just like everything living, they need air and space to breathe under the cap along with their billions of friends. The last problem is that when the skins rise above the liquid, they dry out and can get moldy, and we don't want that. So, we want to keep them wet. Also, most of the flavor is in the skins, so we want them in contact with the juice as much as possible. So, we 'punch down' two to three times per day.

"Go sanitize your arms, your hands and this," the Winemaker said, handing Joe a five-foot-long stainless-steel paddle. "Remember, Winemaking Rules number one, two, three... and four, five, six, seven, eight: 'ANYTHING that touches grapes must be sanitized!'"

The Winemaker pulled back the plastic covering of the first bin. Joe felt a wave of warmth as the heavenly aroma overpowered him. The must was bubbling, and seemed to be alive.

"It is alive," the Winemaker said as if reading Joe's mind. "It is full of life, a whole ecosystem that is living, thriving, multiplying and creating something magical. Our job is to nurture the natural process - because we have very little control over it. Remember that, Joe: we have very little control over anything in our lives. But tonight, we need to make the yeast happy by keeping them cool and giving them oxygen. We want to stir the vats so that every square inch is mixed and blended. From top to bottom, we want this whole bin mixed up."

Joe stepped up onto a small stool and leaned into his paddle. He pushed and strained and pushed and strained, but couldn't break through the thick cap. Beads of sweat popped from his brow.

The Winemaker smiled. "Joe, you're are approaching the problem all wrong. You are going head-on into a formidable mass. This is 2500 pounds of grapes. You can't just force your way in, you must ease in. I appreciate the enthusiasm, but get real. Rock from left to right while driving the edges of the paddle down into the must. Use your momentum, and once you break through, use the small opening to nibble at the cap. Just like with your problems: you have to constantly nibble away at them or they build up."

It took Joe five minutes to work the paddle through the two-foot thick cap, but eventually he did, sweat and all. Then he slowly nibbled at the edges, as advised. After twenty minutes, he had thoroughly mixed the bin.

"Great job, Joe. Only nine more to go."

At 4:00 am Joe crashed heavily into his bed, only to be woken at 5:00 by the rude alarm clock. Winemaking sucks, was his only thought as he splashed cold water on his tired face.

The early morning air blew through the dining room window as Joe positioned himself in his chair and sat for meditation. His back was straight but relaxed, hands resting on his lap. He sat with intention and calmness. Over the last few days he had performed this ritual, and it had started feeling good. He couldn't explain the feeling, but it just felt right.

He started with counting his breaths. His mind stilled and his breathing slowed until the monkeys started screaming, Joe, you are never going to be much. Just face it and suck it up. We don't care about your dreams or ambitions; we are fine just cashing the paycheck.

With a clenched jaw and firm determination, Joe said, "NO."

He thought about how fun the Crush Crew was: working hard, learning by doing, sweating, but joking, laughing and making a real visible difference. Then he thought about the maze he worked in: the constant stream of supervisors, objectives, goals, and demands. He worked not for a passion, but just a paycheck. Something was wrong, and he knew it.

He thought about his terroir – what it would be, and what it would look like – and then he fell into a vivid dream while sitting in meditation. It was cold and misty. Crinkled frosted grass marked each footstep. A sea of granite tombstones covered the field. In front of Joe was a simple stone that read "Here Lies Average Joe." He awoke in a panic, cold sweat running down his face. His heart was pounding not with excitement, but with fear. This was not the way he wanted his story to end.

CHAPTER 5

"I don't want to be 'Average Joe,'" he exclaimed to the Winemaker.

"But you are, Joe... unless you change your life and begin to follow your passions."

"Change what? I don't want to change. What if I change and mess things up even more than I already have?"

"Joe, I don't think that is even possible. Remember, change is natural. It always happens. Grapes are converted to wine. We are born, grow old and eventually die. Friends come and friends go. But there are only two things that never change."

"What's that?"

"Paying taxes and knowing change will happen." Both men let out a deeply felt, hearty laugh, breaking the tension.

The Zen Winemaker picked up a single grape from a bunch and held it out to Joe.

"This single grape can change the world!" he declared.

"What? How can a single grape change the world?"

"Each wine grape has two or three seeds in it. Out of a single seed, a whole vine will grow. Each vine can then produce over 5,000 more seeds every year. Those 5,000 vines can produce over 25,000,000 vines. Their children can produce over 125 billion vines. Not bad for a simple grape, huh?

"Within each grape is a seed. It is perfect and has all the required parts to grow an entire vine. You, Joe, have a seed within you, and you also have all the required parts to grow and prosper. You can also change the world!"

"I can't even change a car tire. I don't think I could change anything. You know, do anything important, like you do."

"The grape does not know it can change the world, yet it can, just as you can too. You just can't see it yet. Want to learn something new?"

Pulling himself up with a forced smile, Joe said, "Rock on Zen Master."

Glass clinked and two glasses swooped onto the black marble bar. "Are you ready to learn the Zen Steps of Wine tasting Joe?"

"What are the ten steps, oh Master?" Joe mocked.

"No, smart ass, the ZEN steps are: seeing, swirling, smelling, sipping, savoring and selling. Tonight, we are only going to talk about the first Zen step, seeing."

"But seeing, swirling, smelling, sipping, savoring and selling all start with S, not Z. That's not very *zenish*."

"Grasshopper, yin and yang," the Winemaker replied as he swished his hands from the shape of an S to that of a Z: symmetrical, opposite. A bottle was grabbed and two glasses were filled. "Grasshopper, tonight we learn that our eyes deceive us and we need to learn the truth."

"The truth about what? And why do you call me Grasshopper?"

"You need to learn many things, Grasshopper. And the reason you are called Grasshopper is that you have shown me that you know so very little about life, and a master must help you become a master yourself. So, Grasshopper, look at your wine and tell me what you see."

Joe picked up his glass and did what felt natural: he held it up to the light. In the reflection of his glass were myriad reflections and a kaleidoscope of colors. The world looked distorted and funny.

"Joe, what are you seeing?"

"I see everything, all these colors, and reflections. It's kind of cool."

"But Joe, what is the true and only color of the wine."

Joe stopped and looked. For the first time he saw and realized that as he moved the glass, the colors in the glass changed. Different backgrounds looked different through the wine. Confused, Joe said, "I don't know."

"Neither do a lot of people. Most people – well, almost all people – tend to think that what they see is real."

"Of course, what they see is real. Reality is right there in front of you. How can you miss it?"

"Joe, can you truly see the wine? What exact color is it? What does it look like?"

"I have no idea; the wine just reflects different colors and patterns."

"Then you are not seeing the truth. You are not seeing reality, just an illusion created by your mind and by the environment. Do not ever think that this illusion is real. It is not, and your lesson tonight is to understand this. This understanding will serve you well in life.

"Have you ever tried on sunglasses at the drug store? Some look good, some look bad, some are too big or too small. Some make everything yellow, or blue or gray. None allows us to see what is real.

"Every experience in life paints color on the lenses in your mind, and that is what you believe is 'real.' Realizing that someone else with a different pair of sunglasses would see a different reality, how can two different reals then be real? Obviously - one must be fake, or both are fake. If both are fake then everything is fake – insofar as everyone's perception of the 'real' is different.

"Realizing this can simplify your life tremendously!"

The Winemaker took up his glass, holding it about six inches above a clean white surface. He rotated it through ninety degrees, from ten o'clock to two, peering through it as he did so. Then he looked straight down through the glass, the wine and onto the white surface, motionless.

Joe took his glass and did the same. The wine was now a golden yellow, with hints of straw and a touch of green. Over the blank surface, there were no reflections or distortions.

"Now Joe, you can begin to see and understand the wine. Remove the background noise and you can truly see the wine. You can learn from the wine and the wine will tell you its story if you know how to listen with your eyes.

"This applies to everything we see; everything is distorted by background noise. This noise comes from the surroundings and our own experiences and biases. You see what you look for and ignore what you are not interested in. Reality is right in front of you, but you can't see it, and if you do see it, it is probably wrong. But we are going to fix that.

"If everyone could see reality, magicians would be out of business. Their craft depends on being able to trick the eye, to cause it to believe one thing and not another. Magicians make the impossible real, and so do most people. People are experts at creating, maintaining and fulfilling an illusion: 'My life will be better when I get a new job.' 'If I won a million dollars my problems would all go away.' 'If I just stay in a bad relationship for a bit longer, it will get better.' 'That person will change their habits if I pressure them.' 'If I do what Jones does, then all my problems will go away.'

"You see, people build these fantasy worlds. They live in the past, fostering memories of times long gone by, or they dream of possibilities that will arrive in the future, or they worry about events that may never happen. When reality is staring them right in the face this very moment – the only reality to see is right now.

"Are you still meditating Joe?"

"Yeah, every morning for ten minutes."

"That's good. You will soon begin to see the noise, the confusion, the assumptions and the biases that you have accumulated up in the attic of your brain. One day you will learn how to clean up your attic, throw away all those false assumptions, and begin to see the world with the eyes of a baby. Babies do not have all the stored-up trash in their attics, so they see what is real.

"Now what do you see in your wine glass?"

"The wine has a light golden color – or maybe a dark straw. It's clear and sparkles under the light. In the deepest part, it's darker than the edge, which is almost clear."

"That's great Joe, you are starting to master seeing reality. What most people do not understand is that a master of wine can look at a glass of wine, and just by its appearance begin to identify what type of wine it is, where it comes from, the quality and how old the wine is."

"How can they do that?"

"The color is the first clue as to what type of grape was used to produce this wine. In this case, the wine is light golden with a slight darkening in the deepest part. This suggests that this wine comes from a white grape varietal and the wine was not aged in a lot of oak, which would give it a deeper hue. The rim is indicating the wine is young, under two years old. The wine is clear without any flocculation, so it was either made with care or filtered – I think made with care. Because of the color, I think this was grown in a cooler climate. So, my final guess is - 2017 Chardonnay from Santa Maria Valley in California."

"Amazing, how did you do that?"

Holding up a bottle of 2017 Santa Maria Valley Chardonnay, the Winemaker said with a sheepish smirk, "I made this wine. But if you look at each wine you sample and remember what it looked like and compared it against all other wines that you have tried, you begin to understand the subtle differences between each varietal and each region.

"Instead of scrutinizing reality, people tend to categorize objects, which blurs reality. Suppose you go to the dog park. There are big dogs and small dogs, white dogs and brown dogs, but they are all dogs. So, our brain says, 'Dogs have four legs, bark, wag their tails and are man's best friend.' As soon as we do this, we no longer see reality, we see a stereotype of a dog in our mind and we lose reality. What you need to do is to begin to unlearn all that you have learned and look at the world with baby eyes."

For the first time in a long time, Joe took the time to looked at the scenery on the way home. He realized that even though he had driven on these roads hundreds – if not thousands – of times, he had never really taken the time to just look at his surroundings. He lived his life in his head, in what the Winemaker called a false reality.

Wispy clouds were turning pink in the evening sun. The fog formed a wall close to the ocean as the marine layer moved in. Large planes left contrails crossing and fading in the autumn sky. Joe realized as he pulled into the driveway that the typical noise in his head had been silent the entire drive. For the last ten minutes, he had been in the moment, seeing with clear eyes what was right in front of him.

"Mary, when did the neighbors paint their house?"

"Two years ago, why?"

"Oh, nothing. Just never noticed, that's all. What's for dinner?"

Lucy was sitting in her booster chair happy as could be, swinging her plump little legs and banging her spoon and fork on the tray. Mary rounded the corner with a big bowl of steaming stir-fry. The food looked amazing; the bright colors of the steamed vegetables piled on brown rice. Joe's mouth began to water in anticipation, his eyes eating the food morsel by morsel.

As Mary sat, Joe looked deeply into her amber eyes. Long locks of curly hair framed the smooth skin of her face, with its sculpted nose and delicate jaw.

"Mary, you are the most beautiful woman in the entire universe."

Mary glowed and did so again after Lucy went to bed that evening.

The next morning at work, Joe spent more time looking around his office. People with long faces passed by his cubicle, flashing faint polite smiles. The managers huddled here and there, each glancing out with conspiracy in their eyes. Something was happening, and it didn't feel good. The more Joe looked – really looked – the more clearly he saw that the merger was getting closer - and that it might not be good for him.

There was a feeling in Joe's gut that just wouldn't go away. A nervousness deep down within his core. It was faint, but it was there. Lurking, a silent scream he couldn't understand yet. He recalled the Winemaker's story about seeing.

The Winemaker locked eyes with Joe and began, "Lacking any clear direction, I stepped off the stage with my bachelor's degree in my hand. I started in 1986 with a small company that installed solar-powered water heating systems and did some home improvements. Starting as a draftsman, I was promoted

29

to lead foreman within three months. Why? Because the lead foreman was in jail. Within a month the president was arrested for attempted rape. Within days the company collapsed, but the 'good' news was that the lead salesman made me a proposition: 'Hey, this company is funded by an angel investor. I'm tight with him and can get operating cash until we make it big! We can do it ourselves. What do you think?'

"Being ambitious and naive, I said 'Sure, what could possibly go wrong?!'

"After two years without a paycheck, my dreams broken, I found out that my partner had embezzled hundreds of thousands of dollars, leaving the company gutted.

"So, Grasshopper, what should I have seen?"

All Joe could respond with was, "I guess we see what we want to see?"

For the next few days, Joe observed what was happening around the office. That feeling in his gut kept rumbling. The writing was on the wall – but no one chose to read it. Everyone just passed it by with the false hope of security and luck. But the more Joe watched, the more concerned he became. He began to see clearly how he had chosen to wear blinders, to ignore the signs and to live in a fantasy world, hoping that things would get better and that this merger would make it all alright. With clear eyes and a new understanding, he simply didn't believe that false story anymore.

Joe realized that change was coming, and since he was not part of the decision process, he was just going to be blown around like a leaf in the wind. He had to do something – not just for himself, but for Mary and Lucy.

Each night he awoke with fits of panic, haunted by vivid dreams: adrift in a stormy sea, the mainsail ripped, the huge swells as the storm approached, lightning flashing in the distance. Adrift, out of control and tossed around, helpless and weak.

Darius Miller

CHAPTER 6

It was 10:15 am. With shades drawn and lights off, the winery tasting room was dark. Frustrated and depressed, Joe had called in sick with a stomach bug. He figured no one wanted to be around someone exploding from either end, and he desperately needed a mental health day off.

The Winemaker was behind the bar, swirling a glass of white wine and gazing into it as Joe walked in. The winery smelled amazing, thick with aromas of fermentation. Joe fondly brushed his hands across the covered bins he had helped destem just a few days ago.

"How are our babies doing?"

"Simple and smooth, just like Mother Nature intended. Our job is just to help her out. To nurture the process and not screw things up. She is an old pro at this kind of stuff, and even after thousands of years of making wine, we are just beginning to understand her. She can be fickle, and she always wins.

"Fermentation is a natural process. The vines convert sunlight into sugar. Yeast converts sugar into alcohol. Acetobacter converts alcohol into vinegar, which is the end of the process. A winemaker's job is to monitor and nurture this process so that we end up with wine and not with vinegar – unless you want to make salad dressing," he chuckled. "So how is life going?"

The question brought Joe up short. He began a few times to try to explain, but had to stop, unable to find the words. Finally, he said, "I don't know. Not so good, but not so bad. I am starting to see things differently now. Well, I should say, to see things as they actually are. I know that I have been living in a fog or a dream or whatever you want to call it. I didn't appreciate the good things and tried to ignore the bad things, but that is getting harder and harder. It's like a rabbit hole: it just goes on and on and I feel there isn't a way to get out of it. The more I see, the more frustrated I become. Sometimes I wish I had never stepped into Koi Zen Cellars. I could have just lived in my little fantasy bubble and moved on.

"I know that's a cop-out, and I'm just trying to blame you for my problems, but I just don't see how to get out of this mess I'm in. There is so much going on that is out of my control, I'm constantly panicked and not sure what to do. What should I do?"

"Sorry Joe, I make wine, not people. Have you ever heard the ancient parable about the elephant?"

"No, I don't think so."

"A king brought in eight blind men and an elephant, and asked the blind men to describe it to him. Each touched a different part of the elephant. The first blind man touched the head and said it was a great bowl. The second touched the tusk and said it was a plow blade to cut the earth. The third touched the ear and said it was a tool to separate the grain from the chaff. The fourth touched the trunk and said it was a pipe for water. The fifth touched the leg and said it was a pillar. The sixth touched the back and said it was a large worktable. The seventh touched the tail and said it was a pestle to grind herbs and spices. And the eighth touched the tip of the tail and said it was an artist's brush.

"Each man touched the elephant, though each man thought it was something other than what it was. Even though they were blind, they saw something different, much like you Joe. You have a limited perspective, and maybe that needs to be addressed.

"Today Joe, we are going to learn how to swirl, the second Zen Step of Winetasting."

With the mention of sipping wine – even at 10:30 in the morning – Joe was all in.

The Zen Winemaker snatched two glasses from behind the bar, grabbed a bottle of Cabernet Sauvignon and poured a small splash into each glass. Joe went to grab the glass. The Winemaker raised his palm with authority, indicating to Joe to stop.

"We are now going to talk about the second Zen Step of Winetasting which is swirling. This is one of the most important steps in appreciating both wine and life, and yet so few people do this."

Holding up a bottle, the Winemaker continued, "Joe, the wine in this bottle is alive. It is filled with microbes and chemical reactions and myriad other things, but it has been trapped in a bottle for a long time, unable to breathe.

"Did you know that humans can survive for three weeks without food, three days without water, but only about three minutes without air? Living things need to breathe, dead things do not. Remember this, Joe. It is one of the most important things you can learn. You need to be able to breathe, not only with your lungs, but with your mind, body, and spirit. Otherwise, you will die."

Joe wondered if this was why a little part of him did feel dead inside.

The Winemaker lifted his glass and clumsily attempted to swirl the glass. The wine sloshed from side to side and almost spilled out. He looked up and said, "Even after thirty years of practice, I still can't hold a glass of wine and swirl it properly. Some people are expert air swirlers, but not me. I am what you call a table swirler."

He set his glass on the bar top and then placed two fingers on the base, one on each side of the stem. Then, starting slowly and building a rhythm, he began to move the base of the glass in a small circle. The wine swirled, creeping up the sides of the glass and painting it a burgundy color. A smile washed over the Winemaker's face. Joe could see that this simple act gave him tremendous joy.

"You see Joe," he said, "some people can do it this way" – he snatched up his glass and sloshing it around in the air – "and others can do it this way" – he placed it back on the bar top. "But either way, it gets the job done. There are always multiple ways to approach a problem. Many people fail to see it that way and think that their way is the only way. This leads to disagreements, arguments, fights, divorces, and wars.

"If people could only realize this simple fact, that there are always multiple solutions, I think the world would be a vastly better place."

Joe picked up his glass and tried to swirl. Likewise, the wine sloshed uncontrollably all over the place. He then put the glass down on the bar and, holding the stem, began to swirl. The wine began to rise up the side of the glass. Then there was a snap, and Joe was left holding only the stem and the bowl of the glass; the base remained on the bar. Embarrassed, he looked up to meet compassionate eyes.

"Joe, even if there are many ways, some ways are still not right. Next time, hold the base and the stem will never break." The Winemaker took the broken glass from Joe and poured the contents into a new glass.

"I'm so sorry."

"Joe, don't be sorry. You just learned the most important lesson of the day. You learned that you must try something different; sometimes it works and sometimes it does not, but after a while, you learn what does work and what does not work. This is the only true learning we can ever achieve. Do not be afraid to fail. It is the best teacher you can ever find.

"You can get information from a book or a teacher, but you only truly learn things by doing them. When I was in college, I thought I could learn calculus by reading a book, but that did not work. After failing the class, I realized I needed to do the homework, practice my skills and learn by doing. This also applies to listening to other people, other views, other news. You do not know anything until you have experienced it yourself.

"So many people waste so much energy walking around saying, 'They should do this in the Middle East,' or 'They should do this or that to control immigration,' or 'This is how we should solve the problem with homelessness,' without ever actually experiencing it themselves.

"They are failing to see, to be in that situation – to walk in their shoes, to experience it first hand. In my humble opinion, ask the homeless how to solve the homeless problem and that solution would probably work far better than one created by some political figurehead. But that is just the opinion of a simple winemaker."

Joe placed two fingers on the base, and within moments had the wine swirling like a pro. "Look, I'm a wine connoisseur now, but why are we doing this? Is it just to look cool or what?"

"It does look cool, and it does look like you are a pro, but it serves a very important purpose, a purpose you will learn another day. For now, practice your swirling and enjoy your wine."

The sun had just passed its zenith when Joe walked through the front door surprising Mary.

"Joe, darling, are you OK? Is everything okay at that office?"

"I never went to the office this morning. Called in sick with a stomach bug. I don't have one, I just needed some time to get my thoughts together. So, this morning I went to the coffee shop to think about my/our situation and tried to figure things out. I didn't get very far. Well, I actually got a little frustrated, so I went to the winery – you know, Koi Zen."

"I don't think drinking is going to solve any of our problems. That's a very bad habit to start."

"I didn't go to drink. I went for some advice, from the Zen Winemaker. The way he explains things helps me see things differently. Anyway, grab Lucy: let's go stroll down Main Street. It's a beautiful fall day. The air is crisp and I need to swirl my mind a little."

"Swirl your mind?"

"Yeah, I'll explain on our walk."

"But Lucy is still napping and I'm trying to find any job possible…"

"That's exactly why we need to take a walk."

Main Street was practically empty as they strolled along, Joe pushing Lucy in her stroller and holding hands with Mary. They walked leisurely, gazing at the shops, each different, each trying to catch the consumer's eye – each trying to make a buck.

"So, Mary, what turns you on?"

"Joe, we're in public, and you know what turns me on – that's why we have Lucy."

"That was one great night, but no. I meant: what do you want to do? What type of job are you looking for?"

"Anything. Anything that I can find that helps to pay the bills and is flexible enough to give me time to look after Lucy."

"But, given the chance, what is your ideal job – you know, the thing that inspires you or drives you? We have been walking down Main Street, and every shop it different. We have a bakery, a dentist, a doctor, an insurance company, a pre-school..."

"A teacher, that's what I want to be. I know it sounds crazy, but I really don't like doing marketing for clients. Everyone is pushing why their product is better than the next and why you must buy now and how it's all about the almighty dollar.

"Lucy is just a baby, but one day she will go to school and learn all about life. I want it to be a good experience for her. I want her education to be the best it can be, and I think I can help with that. I think I can make a real difference.

"You know, teaching is very similar to sales. You have to pitch a concept to an often-unwilling client, a student who often doesn't care about classes and homework and such. But you must sell it to them, you must encourage them to want to learn. I think I can help."

"A teacher! Wow, I never knew you felt so strongly about this."

"But it's just a dream. A dream that will never happen. I would have to get my teaching credentials, which takes time, and we have bills to pay – and you might be 'right-sized' out of a job..."

"Now whose cup is full?"

"Speaking of being full, I have to use the ladies room, I'll be right back."

With Lucy in tow, Joe found an empty bench. He spun the stroller viewing his beautiful child. Immediately his heart was full of love for his daughter. She was so special and perfect in every respect and brought him boundless joy. Why could Lucy and Mary invoke such strong emotions and his work didn't? Why was he disengaged and unwilling to move forward?

His mind wandered, thinking about the world his daughter would grow up in. Would she be healthy and happy? Would she find love and companionship? Would she fulfill her life with passion and follow her dreams, or would she be directionless and lacking purpose like he was? He desperately wanted his daughter's life to be filled with hope and happiness though he didn't know how. With no plan, he just hoped he would not let his family down in the next few months, but his mood brightened as Mary approached.

"I went to the winery today because I felt really confused about everything, and then I learned about swirling wine. Strangely, this is why we are now walking down Main Street in the middle of the day talking about you being a teacher.

"The Zen Winemaker taught me how to swirl wine, and how it is important to mix things up. So many people are trapped in a little bubble they call life. They have the same routine, they eat the same foods, watch the same shows on TV, they hang out with the same friends. It's all routine. It's like being trapped in a bottle. Just going round and round – like zombies.

"The Winemaker talked about the importance of looking at life from a different perspective – just like swirling wine, which swirls all around, 360 degrees. And by doing this you can look at your problems, your situation, and your options differently. You see things from different perspectives. Being aware of your options is very liberating, and a little scary."

"Why would it be scary?"

"Because often you see the truth when you actually look around, and you might not like what you see – especially about yourself. This is why so many people put their heads in the sand and pretend that everything is okay when in fact it isn't. For example, you said your dream job would be to be a teacher, but you also told me all the reasons you can't do this – so you just go around and around – never really getting where you want to go. I think you would make an excellent teacher – let's make it happen."

"But, what if —"

Joe simply held up his palm, gesturing for her to stop. "But what if you succeed? Wouldn't that be super cool?"

Joe, Mary, and Lucy spent the rest of the afternoon strolling in town, laughing, chatting and having a good time. Joe could feel the stroller wheel click on the sidewalk with a hypnotic, meditative cadence. His mind drifted to the winery and all that he had learned.

Out of the blue, Joe started, "Did you know that the French use the word 'élevage' to describe the process when a wine is maturing? It means to grow up or to mature. Wine ages differently in different conditions. Bulk aging happens when it is in tanks or barrels, and then there is bottle aging. Each is different and gives a different nuance to the wine. Just like wine, our environment will affect how we change and mature.

"Once the wine goes into the bottle, however, much less oxygen gets into it. It can vary depending on the closure that is used. What you want is a little oxygen over a long period of time. This helps age the wine and helps it balance and smooth out. But once you open a bottle of wine, you expose it to a lot of air, and you need to help it breathe. This is why it's important to swirl the wine. You want to let it breathe: to expand and release all the pent-up flavors it developed by being locked inside of a bottle.

"When you swirl a glass of wine, you are incorporating a ton of oxygen into the wine, letting it breathe and release its true character. If you don't swirl your wine, then it remains all pent up and reserved, never allowed to express its true potential.

"I guess that's a lot like people. We are often trapped in a bottle – or a bubble – and can't breathe. There is this invisible wall around us that doesn't allow us to expand, just like a cork. It isn't until something happens, like pulling a cork out, that we can see a new perspective. It allows us to breathe and to express ourselves the way we were meant to be."

"To be honest, I feel like wine forgotten in a bottle, all locked up and no place to go. And the sad part is, I am just waiting for someone else to decide my fate."

"And you learned all this from the winery?"

"Yeah. The Winemaker's advice resonates with me. And it is not just the words - I have seen people change. That place changes lives."

Raising an eyebrow, Mary asked, "Is it helping you?"

"I think so. I am still learning a whole lot, but it is helping me figure this whole thing out."

"I see a change in you also. You need to follow a new path and if the winery can help – then go for it, but please watch the day drinking."

Joe lit up giving Mary a big hug and kiss seeing the understanding in her eyes.

CHAPTER 7

"Sorry Larry, but my stomach bug is back, can't make it work today." Joe hung up the phone with a smirk on his face as he looked at the email:

Hey Crush Crew:

Today we will be pressing ten tons of Pinot Noir, hope you can make it. We will be starting at 9:00 am, and for those of you who have that "work" thing going on, stop on by when you get off. I am sure we will be going late.

Cheers,

Zen Winemaker

Taking the last sip of cold coffee, he quickly scribbled a note to Mary, grabbed his keys and out of the door he flew. Every time he headed off to the winery, he felt different. He had a purpose and enjoyed being a Crush Crew Student under the tutelage of the Zen Winemaker.

The winery was buzzing with excitement when he arrived. A small crew was busy moving the fermentation bins and sanitizing the equipment they would be using. Pungent aromas of fermenting grapes filled the air, and Joe was about to experience the birth of baby wine.

The Winemaker was off to the side, testing samples of wine from each bin to verify that everything was ready for the pressing.

"Hey Joe, sour stomach again?" he grinned.

"Yep, but it cleared up as soon as I got into my car to drive over here. What's going to happen today? I haven't pressed before."

"These grapes have been fermenting for eleven days now. I am testing each bin to demine how much residual sugar is left in the wine, using a hydrometer. The hydrometer measures the specific gravity of the juice and from that, we can calculate how much sugar is left." The Winemaker handed Joe a graduated cylinder filled with juice and a long glass instrument that looked like a pregnant thermometer.

"Joe, you remember rule number one?"

"Yes: anything that touches the wine must be sanitized. I have sanitized my hands and arms, and even took a shower this morning." Joe put down the cylinder and carefully washed the instrument.

Smiling, the Winemaker said, "Okay, now carefully lower the hydrometer into the cylinder and give it a gentle spin. Spinning will remove any air bubbles that cling to the hydrometer and will give us an accurate reading." Joe did so, and the hydrometer gently spun and bobbed up and down in the liquid, eventually settling to rest.

"On the shaft of the hydrometer is a scale. What does the scale read where the wine touches the hydrometer?"

"It looks like -1.25," Joe said.

"Perfect. The hydrometer is a very accurate way to measure sugar content in the wine. When we start fermentation, the grapes have 23% to 26% sugar content. As the yeast converts the sugars to alcohol, the hydrometer will read a lower number until it goes negative. Any reading below zero indicates that the wine is dry, meaning it does not have any remaining sugar.

"If there is any residual sugar in the wine, there is always a chance that the wine will spontaneously begin to referment in the bottle. This is not good. The yeast will produce carbon dioxide and will begin to push the corks out.

"One of our first batches of wine was produced from a grape called Symphony. This wine is often produced off-dry, meaning it still has some sugar present. After we put it into the bottle, we noticed that it started getting sparkly. Then it became bubbly, and then it started pushing out corks. In a panic, we notified everyone who had bought the wine and told them to drink it immediately. Everyone enjoyed the semi-sparkling wine, except for a good friend of ours who did not heed our advice.

"Some months later, while watching TV, they heard a pop, and a geyser of wine shot out from their wine rack. We all laugh about it now, but at the beginning of the winery, we were worried. We still get worried about our wines. Opening a winery was a big scary step and every little thing spooked us.

"But you know what? It was all worth it. All the stress, the late nights, the financial commitment was so much better than my former life. But that is a tale for another day."

The winery was buzzing with Crush Crew students emptying pail after pail of must from the fermentation tanks into the press. Standing about six feet tall and ten feet long, the press looked like a giant shiny stainless-steel hotdog lying on its side with a large metal tray below it.

The hatch clanked shut and a sweaty student jumped down from the stool and began programing the press. One button controlled the rotation, another the pressure, and other controls determined which program to run. Within a few moments, the press began to rotate and a rush of air was heard. Moments later a waterfall of wine began to fall from the press into a tray below, filling it with a purplish burgundy-colored wine.

A transfer pump whirled and the wine was pumped from the tray into awaiting barrels, which were neatly stacked in a long row waiting to receive the wine.

The Winemaker held a plastic cup under the torrent of wine and took a sip. His face was neutral as he swished the wine in his mouth, then he smiled. "Want to taste baby wine, Joe?"

"Sure," he said, taking the cup. It tasted like wine, but rough, unfinished, and not very tasty at all. He winced a little, and looked at the Winemaker with questioning eyes.

"Joe, think of when Lucy was first born. Like most babies, she was probably wrinkly with a misshapen head and covered in muck. Not very attractive, but within a few hours, their color changes and they slowly mature into a beautiful person. Baby wine is the same way. It's ornery, it cries, it makes a mess and generally throws fits. But give it proper nurturing and time, and it will mellow into the nectar of the gods." The cup was passed around the crew, and everyone nodded with approval.

"Joe, you can't expect immediate perfection in what you do. You need time to refine, to grow and adapt, and step by step sand off the rough corners and polish it to perfection. It is unwise to get frustrated too quickly when you try something new. Remember this simple lesson and it will save you countless hours of stress and frustration.

"When I was younger, I would always estimate the time it took to do something as if I were an expert. One day I was replacing the brakes on my car. I figured it would take thirty minutes to complete each wheel. The first time I did it, it took over four hours – per wheel. A horrible underestimation. But after doing it a few times, I could replace the brake pads in thirty minutes or less. The lesson is that you need to allocate extra time in the beginning. You need time to figure things out and to learn all those lessons that you never thought about. Remember this when you make your big change."

"What big change?" Joe asked.

But the Winemaker had wandered away to check on the progress of the press.

###

An hour later, there was a giant whoosh and the press became still. The crew immediately removed the catch pan and replaced it with an empty macro bin. The door of the press was flung open and the drum was rotated. Out fell hundreds of pounds of pomace, the remains left after pressing the wine. The pomace filled half the bin. During the whole process, 500 liters of wine had been extracted – enough to fill 650 bottles of wine. After all the pomace was dumped out of the press, the crew replaced the catch pan under the press and began bucketing must into the press, filling it up again.

Joe fingered the dried pomace and asked what they did with it. The Winemaker responded, "I have some friends who use it for composting. There is a huge amount of nutrients in the pomace and it is a great organic filler. In some places, they feed it to cows and chickens. Each dried-up berry here is saturated in alcohol. Maybe this is why California has happy cows," he joked.

"Joe, it's very important to Koi Zen and its community to be as mindful of the environment as possible. By composting this pomace and the rachis – the stems that hold the berries on – we are giving back to Mother Earth for the bounty that she has given us. Another area that we are mindful of is the use of water. My daughter, who is a civil engineer, has taught me the importance of water conservation, so we try to minimize our use as much as possible. The average winery uses 5.5 gallons of water for every gallon of wine produced. At Koi Zen we have minimized this down to a mere 6 oz per gallon – that's less than 1% of the average winery.

"It is amazing how, when you are mindful about your surroundings, small actions can lead to great improvement. This applies to all of life. Hopefully, you are being mindful of your actions, Joe."

Nodding, Joe knew he was trying, but still had a long way to go. He was still a young grasshopper.

Joe stood fingering the pomace, amazed at the efficiency of the whole operation. Everyone was getting the job done quickly, safely and efficiently while laughing, chatting and having a great time. The green shade of envy grew in his heart: he so wished that his job was even 5% as enriching and interesting as this.

Joe began to realize that there was a change coming – a big change. A tingle of excitement spread through his soul and he smiled at how far he had already traveled. Only weeks ago, the thought of a big change would have evoked mental anguish, dread, and resistance. But something had changed within him, and he was glad.

He sanitized his hands and arms and jumped in on the bucket assembly line, scooping up fermented berries and passing the bucket to the pressman, who dumped each bucket into the press. Some 1500 pounds later, the press was full and the whole press process began again. The crew washed up, sat down and began chatting.

The crew jested with each other, told stories and shared problems. They provided support and guidance without judgment, and always with compassion for the other person. Even though these people came from different backgrounds and experiences, they all came together to share parts of their lives. It was a truly remarkable experience.

Joe sat to the side of the group, not knowing how to fit in but yearning too.

"Grasshopper, has the Winemaker shared the secret of life with you yet?"

"The secret of life? No, I don't think so. What is it?"

"Oh Grasshopper, you will soon find out. Everyone does – some sooner, some later, but you will – if you listen close enough."

Joe sat back and wondered what this all meant – somehow, he knew he would soon find out.

The night air was cool as the dashboard clock flipped to 11:43 pm. Joe drove home, dirty, sticky, smelling like a wine bottle, and with the largest possible grin on his face. Exhausted and sore, he fell into a deep sleep.

Five hours later his alarm drove him to the shower. The hot water washed across his sore muscles and the dread of his workday began to rise. His hands were stained dark reddish and every crease on his palm was highlighted. No matter how much he scrubbed, the wine stains would not wash off. How am I going to explain this when I was supposed to have a stomach bug? He wished he could stay in the shower all day and just rinse all his problems away, but just like the stain on his palms, his problems wouldn't simply wash down the drain.

Darius Miller

CHAPTER 8

Joe jumped in his car only to find the entire steering wheel sticky from the previous night's activities. He smiled and wished he was headed to the winery and not the office. Two blocks away from his house, a car almost cut him off. Instead of overreacting he just smiled, grateful for not getting involved in an incident, and thought, 'They must have some very important business to attend to. No harm was done, move on Joe.' This brought a huge smile to his face. Maybe, just maybe he was beginning to become a better person after all.

Trying to explain his wine-stained hands to Larry, his boss, involved a little fib, but he was welcomed back and congratulated for getting over his 'stomach bug.' My boss congratulates me for getting over a fake illness but hasn't complimented me in years for the long hours and exceptional work I do. I need to get out of here.

All morning, click after click Joe searched the wanted ads. He had no clue what he was looking for, or what he was even qualified for. All his life he had done what he was told to do, taking any job that would pay the bills. Living in a house that he didn't really like, but having no ambition to find someplace better. After a few hours, he realized that most of his life he had operated on autopilot.

Other than Mary and Lucy, he had no passions, no hobbies, no interests: just the same old grind day after day, month after month, year after year. Even after eight years, he was still in the same job, the same cube, pushing the same papers and clicking the same buttons. He had been passed over for a promotion twice, and with the merger and restructuring looming, he knew that his current job was in jeopardy, either by management or for the sake of his sanity.

"Sorry guys, I'm going to skip lunch today. I need to get some fresh air and empty my cup." The air was crisp and Joe felt refreshed. Billowy clouds filled the sky, creating dappled patterns on the sidewalk. The leaves were beginning to change color and some fluttered in the breeze. He walked slowly, aware of each foot lift and footfall. In tune with his body, he walked for half a mile in silent walking meditation. A park bench under a scrub oak tree was open, and he sat watching the light reflect on a nearby pond.

Small breezes caused ripples across the water, breaking up the reflected image as if in a hypnotic kaleidoscope. Idle thoughts drifted in and out of Joe's mind as he sat in silence. The birds chirped and the squirrels raced around, finding acorns to store for the winter and secreting them away in their hiding places. Winter was coming, a new season and a new start – to what, Joe didn't know.

After a few moments, he was engulfed by a crowd of dogs sniffing here and there. He was startled, but a friendly face smiled back at him. It was Suzie from Crush Crew. "Hey Joe, fancy meeting you here. Say hi to the gang," she said, pointing at the pack of dogs all tugging on their leashes, looking for something even better to smell or investigate.

She clipped the bundle of leashes to the bench and sat down next to Joe amongst the curious dogs.

"Why the long face? It's such a beautiful day, cool and refreshing. It feels like the seasons are changing. I have been walking this park with the dogs almost every day for about three years now. We know every inch and every smell possible, and no matter how many times we come here, there is always something a little different about the park if you take the time to notice it. You see parents with little kids come and go, first pushing strollers, then holding little hands, and then parents chasing their kids around. Sometimes the day's hot, and others are cool, sometimes still and sometimes breezy. The flowers come and then fade, the leaves turn green, then brown and float away. Always the same, but always slightly different. Know what I mean?"

"Not really, Suzie. It seems that I sit in the same cube day in and day out and that nothing ever changes, just the same old grind day after day. Today I just had to get out of the office and try to clear my head. I just needed a few moments to sit and think."

"I'm sorry, the dogs and I will get out of your hair," Suzie said, as she started to unlatch the leashes.

"No, please stay. It is nice to see a friendly face. You sure do have a lot of dogs."

"Oh, these guys aren't mine, I just walk them every day, just like the mailman, rain or shine. I know what you mean about being stuck in an office. I just hated that, and so here I am now. A completely different person all thanks to the Winemaker."

"The Winemaker? At Koi Zen Cellars – that Winemaker?"

"Yeah, the same. I stumbled into the Crush Crew much the way you did. I was frustrated with my job and the path that I was on. My karma was not aligned properly, and I was on the verge of totally burning out, losing my husband and my mind.

"I was a wreck in all dimensions of my life: my family, my marriage, my work, my addictions, my mind. Everything was a mess, and now, it's all good! I walked away from my job, patched up my relationships, cleaned up some bad habits and am a much happier person than I was then. And I have to thank the Zen Winemaker for helping me out."

"Wow, that sounds like a lot of change. What kind of work did you do before this?"

"I was a corporate lawyer, defending companies against employee lawsuits. I only worked for big companies; they were the only ones who could afford my fees. Not to brag, but before I left law, I was making over $250,000 a year."

"I don't mean to be rude, but how could you walk away from that kind of money for this?" Joe said, pointing to the dogs. "You can't be making much more than a few bucks a day walking dogs."

Suzie let out a huge laugh, startling the dogs who were laying at their feet. She giggled to herself for almost a minute. Joe began to feel embarrassed for whatever it was he had said or done – without being entirely sure what it was. She then looked at Joe with tears in her eyes and said, "Joe, I'm not just a dog walker. I am the CEO and owner of the Zen Dog Supply company. Last year we grossed over $15 million in sales and our products are sold across the States."

Joe blushed, feeling like a fool.

"Joe, I just walk the dogs to get some fresh air, to clear the mind out and get some exercise. Been doing it day in and day out."

"How did you go from being a corporate lawyer to running a dog food company?"

"We do a whole lot more than just dog food. We have dog enrichment programs, toys, and dog training videos. Everything a mindful dog owner would ever need. For thousands and thousands of years, dogs and humans have been friends sharing food, shelter, warmth, and protection, and yet after all that time, very few people understand their dogs. Unfortunately, the dog often gets blamed for bad behavior and is punished when in fact it is the owner who should be punished.

"Our products help people better understand and communicate with their furry friends. We teach people how to enrich the dog's life and in return, the dog is happier, develops fewer issues, and the whole relationship is much more fulfilling for everyone. The bottom line, we teach people how to speak dog."

"Fascinating, kind of like that dog whisperer guy. But how does the Winemaker fit in?"

"I stumbled across Koi Zen Cellars on my way to pick up some pickles, and immediately fell in love with the place. The moment I walked in I felt the serenity, the calmness and that very zen feeling that seemed to permeate the whole place. I fell in love with the staff, the wines, the people, and started spending more and more time there.

"It was early fall. I was asking the wine steward how the wine was made, and he asked if I knew about the Crush Crew, and the classes to teach people how grapes are turned into wine. I jumped on that opportunity as fast as I could, and have been learning and participating for four harvests now.

"Reflecting back, it seems every time I went to Koi Zen, I learned something new about making wine – and more importantly, about myself. I began to see things a little differently and began to take responsibility for my life and my actions. Being a lawyer, I was good at finding fault in others – not so great at seeing it in myself. When it came to me, I just blamed everything on everything but myself. In retrospect, I did a lot of damage to myself and my psyche this way. I was never held accountable for my choices, and I realized that I was on a very slippery steep slope. Every day I would sink a little deeper into a dark part of my mind. I would self-medicate and jump at anything shiny that would lift me up and distract me from how horrible I felt inside.

"So, when I learned about Crush Crew, I was all in 100%. From being on the crew I learned that every action needs to be intentional and done with accuracy and precision. Failing to sanitize just once could ruin a whole batch of wine, and I just didn't want to let anyone down. I wanted to be responsible for my actions. The times I did mess up, the Winemaker simply showed me my mistake or a way to improve without being hostile or judgmental.

"This was such a different way than in the courtroom, which was like a battleground. Each party trying to outwit, sabotage or defeat the other side. It was a very hostile and toxic environment to work in for so many years. By being able to step back and reflect on myself, my attitudes, and my beliefs through meditation and yoga, I realized that I was a jerk to most people. No wonder my relationships with my husband and my friends were on such rocky ground.

"Once I began to see reality, I knew I had to change. I had to become responsible for my actions and to begin to climb out of the hole I had dug for myself. I really needed to start to balance my karma out, so I decided to dedicate my energies to a new and positive direction."

"But why dogs? It seems so far away from your former career."

"I was at a low point and had just joined the Crush Crew when Kathy – you know, the tall lady on the crew – asked me to go with her to the animal shelter. That experience opened my eyes and, at that moment, I knew what I had to do.

"Seeing all of those sad brown eyes staring back at me, I knew I had to make things better for them. I didn't know what to do or how to do it, but some dramatic action was required. Some of the dogs had been abused or neglected. Some were so deathly skinny or had open wounds, and even had ripped ears from fighting.

"Do you know that over 10,000 dogs die each year because they are bred to fight each other in arenas and people actually bet on which dog will kill the other? It's just horrible the atrocities that people do just to have a little excitement. So, the sole purpose of my company is to help people develop a healthy relationship with their furry friends and to spread the word about abuse. Not only dogs but all pets – and people too.

"After my epiphany at the shelter, I talked to the only person who I knew who was nonjudgmental and I hoped for some good advice. That night we were pressing Cabernet Franc and between cycles, I asked the Winemaker for his advice."

"And what did he say?"

"He said the strangest and most powerful thing. He said something I will always remember: 'You know your answer, just do it.' And so, I did. It took a few months to make the transition and to develop the courage to walk away from the courtroom. But I did, and I wish I had done it much earlier. I was scared of walking away from a lucrative life, but I now realize that there are more important things in life than chasing a paycheck.

"I followed my heart and with a newfound perspective, I found all of the passion and energy to make it a reality. He told me, 'What you imagine can become a reality.' And for me it did, and I can't be happier."

"Suzie, that's one heck of a tale. I wish I had one-tenth of your courage and commitment, but I'm just a lowly insurance rep. I don't have the courage to make radical changes like you did."

The winds had calmed, and the pond was still reflecting the moving clouds and glittering sunshine. Suzie picked up a small stone. The dogs became very attentive, as if this was the start of a new game, but she threw thirty feet into the pond. The water rippled and the rings began to spread out into ever larger circles.

"Joe, every action has a reaction. That stone caused the ripples. The ripples will continue on and on. By throwing the stone, I have changed the universe in a very small but perceivable way. Once you realize that every action has a reaction, you can use this to change not only yourself, but the world too. Small actions create small ripples. Large actions make larger ripples. Just make sure you are making the 'right' ripples.

"It was great talking to you Joe, but we have to run: I have a world to change. See you at the winery."

Joe watched Suzie and the pack of dogs happily walk away into the early afternoon sun. Every action has a reaction, he thought, glancing at his watch. Good thing Larry is stuck in a management meeting: I'm really late from my lunch break.

###

Joe packed up early and left, deciding to stop by the winery for a quick sip before heading home. The parking lot was quiet, it being only 4:00 in the afternoon. The sun was beginning to set and a cool breeze was in the air.

Quickly scanning the tasting sheet, he picked the Cabernet Franc, a double gold-winning wine in two well respected international wine competitions. It was his current favorite – if he had to choose just one: they were all excellent.

"Hey Joe, we meet again," Suzie said (without the dogs this time). "Come join me." She slid over on the couch and Joe flopped down with a sigh. "What's up? You looked a little down this afternoon, but now you are just a wreck."

"It's been rough at work lately. We are in the middle of a merger and reorganization; I hate my job, and I'm just so envious of you and what you did. I wish I had just 10% of the courage you had to start your own company. I guess I will just be making money for someone else for the rest of my life."

"I know how you feel, Joe. Before I left the courtroom, I had every toy imaginable. New cars, big houses, fancy clothes – everything and anything that money can buy. And you know what? I hated my life. I felt all slimy inside and every day I had to put on a face and be that tough person. All that mattered was winning the case, no matter how much it went against my spirit. On the other side, my brother has been through some rough patches, and he just can't seem to make any money – he isn't too happy with life either. I don't believe that money is necessarily the thing that makes you happy, but rather what you do with it.

"If your sole mission is to make more, to buy more and to have more, then, in my opinion, you are wasting your life and are on a fool's errand. On the other hand, if you use your money to bring happiness and joy to the world, then sure, make as much as possible and give as much as you can. That's what I do: 20% of all my profits go towards helping put an end to animal abuse."

"But you're an entrepreneur, I'm just Average Joe. I don't have any fancy titles or skills. Heck, I don't even know what I want to do in life other than support my wife and daughter, Mary and Lucy. I'm never going to be anything more than that, I'm afraid."

"Sorry to tell you Joe, but you are probably right: you won't be anything other than poor old Average Joe – unless," she said with a sparkle in her eye, "you change the way you think about yourself and your situation. Remember those ripples we talked about today? You see, those ripples go out into the universe and will forever change the universe. Now, you can send out good ripples, or bad ripples. When you send out good ripples, then the good things happen. When you send out bad ripples, then we generally don't like the results.

"By constantly filling your head with negative thoughts, you are manifesting a negative situation. Change how you see the world, how you think about the world, and the world will magically change for you. There was a very wise man named Lao Tzu who lived about 3,000 years ago and wrote a very powerful book filled with simple advice. He said,

'Watch your thoughts, they become your words; watch your words, they become your actions; watch your actions, they become your habits; watch your habits, they become your character; watch your character, it becomes your destiny.'

"If you tell yourself you are a failure, that's what the universe will manifest – is that what you want Joe?"

Joe hung his head and said, "No, but—"

Her face immediately turned stern and she held up her hand, causing Joe to stop midsentence. "Joe, from now on, there shall be no more 'no buts' allowed in our conversations. If the Winemaker heard you say that, you would get the wrath of zen thrown down on you, Grasshopper."

"Oh, come on, no more Grasshopper. I'll be good, I promise."

"I don't want a promise, Joe. I want you to be the best possible person I know you can be. The better you are, the better Mary and Lucy will be, and the better the whole universe will be. Wouldn't that be just grand?"

"I guess so. But… sorry, I mean, how do you change when you don't even know where you are going, or where you want to go?"

"Then create a vision board."

"What's a vision board?"

"It's a really fun project and I create one every few years. It's so much fun to reflect on the magical path that I have taken.

And it's so easy. Go around your house collecting as many old magazines, newspapers, flyers, and catalogs as you can find. Then, being mindful, just flip through them and rip out the interesting pages, and collect maybe a hundred pages. Give it some time and don't think about what you are doing, just let it happen. It might take a few hours or a few days, but once you have about a hundred, then get a large piece of poster board, about two feet by three feet. Then start going through your stack of pages and pick the best ones, the ones that inspire you. Trim them so they look nice and glue them onto the board wherever you want. There is no right or wrong way, just have fun with it and make a collage of whatever you found. Then, this is the magical part: put your board someplace you will see every day, maybe even twice a day. Maybe on the bathroom wall or in a hallway.

"What you will find out is that the things on that board will start to manifest in your life. That's how I came up with the idea of my pet supply company. On my vision boards, I always had pictures of puppies. When I went to the animal shelter that day, something clicked and I knew what I had to do. I heard the universe screaming at me – 'Do it!' – and I knew that I had to. It was my calling."

That night Joe rummaged around the house, collecting up as many materials as he could find.

Mary was pleased – "Oh good, you're finally cleaning up around here" – until he unloaded them onto the dinner table.

"Hey Mary, let's change the universe and make some vision boards."

"Some what?"

"I'll explain everything."

Armed with glue sticks, paste and scissors, they had soon covered the dining room floor with discarded clippings, shredded magazines, and scraps of paper. Lucy had the best time climbing around the mess, happy that for once she wasn't the one who had made it.

At 8:47, Joe's phone beeped. It was a text message from the Winemaker: "Road trip tomorrow? Leaving at 6:00 am to a Santa Barbara vineyard to pick up grapes. Pack an overnight bag."

At 8:48 Joe texted Larry, "Sorry Larry, but my stomach bug is back. I must be eating some bad eggs or something."

CHAPTER 9

Cold, crisp air filled the pale sky as the first hints of sunlight broke through the high clouds. It was cold, at least for San Diego, as Joe pulled into the parking lot. The truck had been loaded with sanitized picking bins, each strapped and secured for the long haul to Santa Ynez Valley to pick this year's Cabernet Franc grapes. Wisps of steam emerged from the tailpipe. The Winemaker was leaning against the side sipping his early morning tea.

"Morning Joe, so glad that you could make the trip. Still have your stomach bug?"

"Oh wise one, maybe a trip to Santa Barbara will cure it. Why are we leaving so early? Are they picking today?"

"Not today, tonight. The picking crews will show up about 1:00 in the morning and should be done by 4:00. We should be back on the road by 5:00 am."

"So why are we leaving so early then?"

"If you don't mind, we can spend the day checking out some new vineyards that I have my eye on, taste some wine and catch up with a few friends. Sound good?"

With a nod, Joe grabbed his gear and threw it into the back of the truck.

Leaving San Diego, the traffic was light and the road was clear. But seventy miles up the road, when they were approaching Corona, the traffic that had been building slowly came to a standstill.

Joe visibly began to fidget in his seat. The frustration growing within him was plain to see. Eventually, he blurted, "This stupid traffic. It seems whenever you need to get someplace all the buttholes in the world get in your way. It just drives me crazy." The ranting and raving went on for the next two painful miles of stop and go.

"Joe, have you ever heard of Marcus Aurelius?" the Winemaker asked without looking at Joe.

Joe shook his head.

"Marcus Aurelius was the last of the great Roman Emperors. He assumed the throne in 161 AD and was the most powerful man in the world. The Roman empire was vast, and constantly in conflict with foreign lands. Marcus Aurelius was viewed as a well-liked and humble person. It was his custom to reflect on his life each day. He was a great Stoic philosopher and wrote in his private journal his strengths and his weaknesses, and continually strove to live a better life and to be a better ruler. His diaries were published after his death in a book called Meditations.

"Are you familiar with Stoicism?"

"I know the word 'stoic' – you know, to endure pain and suffering without showing it."

"That's right, but Stoicism as a philosophical system goes a bit further than that. It uses reason as a means of developing self-control, and fortitude as a means of overcoming destructive emotions. The idea is that, by becoming a clear and unbiased thinker, you can see the universal truth.

"Marcus Aurelius wrote that the key to happiness is to fundamentally understand that one is not really in control of very much, and that getting all worked up about things that one can't control is just plain stupid. People have this perception that they are in control and waste inordinate amounts of energy trying to control the uncontrollable, or waste inordinate amounts of energy talking about the things they can't control. Marcus Aurelius believed that happiness could be achieved by mastering what is under one's control, rather than rambling about what is not under one's control.

"For example, take the traffic today. No matter how much you talk about it, curse about it, worry about it, think about it, frustrate yourself about it, none of this will change the traffic. All it will do is frustrate you – and frustrate me, with your constant whining about it."

The truck lurched to another stop. The traffic had slowed to a crawl. Joe sat sulking like a scolded schoolboy, frustrated with the traffic, the Winemaker and himself. The more he thought, the more frustrated he became. Eventually, he defiantly blurted out, "I'm in control of myself! Don't tell me I'm not in control, because I am."

"Okay Joe, if you are so in control, then why are you frustrated with me, or the traffic, or your life? You can't control your height, your heart beating, your eyes blinking, your breathing, your hair growing, your reflexes, your cells growing and dying. Joe, you can't control any of the hundreds of processes going on in your body all the time. The chemical balances, the way food is digested, the way muscles respond to impulses from the brain. If you are in control of yourself, then prove it by stopping your heart."

"Stop my heart, I can't do that! I'm talking about my actions. You know what I mean! You are just talking in circles to confuse me."

"You are confusing yourself Joe, not me. If you were in control, then you could choose to stop listening to me and just be quiet for once. Remember what you learned about seeing the wine when wine tasting, and you realized that often you don't see things the way they really are? This is the same. Once you realize what is in your control and what is not in your control, life becomes simpler. However, if you are always operating under the fantasy that you can control what you really can't control, you will live in continual frustration and sadness.

"There is only one thing that you can learn to control, and that is your mind. You can learn how to control your emotions, your views, your attitudes, your attention, and where you focus your energies. Almost everything else is completely out of your control. The sad part is that so many people are living in a fantasy, where they think the past was better than it really was, and that the future will fix all problems. But when they are stuck in the now, they're just miserable. Sound familiar, Joe?"

Joe sat in silence, trying to think of all the things that he had control over. His work: no. Getting a promotion: no. What Mary thought: no. How his friends acted: no. Traffic: no. No matter what he thought he could control, he realized he couldn't.

Within fifteen miles, the traffic had lifted, and so had his spirits. He realized the Winemaker wasn't making fun of him, just pointing out an obvious consideration he had never thought of before.

They were passing through Chino Hills when he asked, "You said that Marcus Aurelius thought that you could find happiness by understanding what you can and can't control. I have been sitting here for the last twenty minutes, and I don't feel so happy realizing that I am completely out of control. How can this make you happy?"

"Once you accept that you have so little external control, you can begin to develop your mind. You can begin to convert those things that frustrate you into things that don't bother you. Do this over and over, and you become happier. Once the fantasy and the illusion of control are lifted, you can begin to focus your energies on bringing true happiness to yourself and the world.

"Joe, ever hear the old joke about the guy who went to the doctor? He said, 'Doctor my arm hurts when I bend it this way.'

The doctor replied, 'Then don't bend it that way.' Okay, bad joke, but you get the point. If you don't like where you are, then instead of trying to force your will on the environment, change yourself. Either accept that it is out of your control, or move. Change locations, get on a different path in life. This is where you do have real control."

Traffic ground to a halt as they approached the 210. Joe could feel his blood pressure rising and his muscles tightening. Conscious of his reaction, he thought deeply about the previous conversation and realized that no matter how mad he got, the traffic would be exactly what it was and that the Winemaker was right: all he could control was how he felt about it.

Traffic was stopped. He glanced over to catch a glimpse of a very attractive young lady. He smiled. Maybe there is something to this whole Stoic thing – and maybe I should be more aware of my surroundings. Hmmm...

Joe started to become excited as they passed through Santa Barbara, knowing that wine country was only about an hour away. The frustrations of the past were drifting away and he began to smile for the first time in hours. "I'm glad you are enjoying the ride, Joe. Once we get to the vineyard, we will drop off the trailer and the bins and then go find some fun."

Darius Miller

CHAPTER 10

Gravel crunched and plumes of dust rose behind the truck as they turned off Baseline Road onto a dirt driveway leading to the vineyard. The outside thermometer read 105 degrees. Out of Joe's window was a large field with squat green plants and a dozen workers tending to the crops. Through the dust, Joe could see that they all wore long-sleeved white paper jumpsuits, gloves, facemasks, goggles, and hats; completely covered from head to toe.

"They're picking jalapeños. The capsicum oil of the pepper can give you severe irritation and burns if you handle them for too long, especially in this heat. If you ever think that your job sucks, just think of these workers who squat in the blistering hot fields day in and day out."

A quarter of a mile down the dirt road stood a tall, twisted, rusty gate that barely held together. "Joe, go open the gate. The staging area is just up to the left." As he swung the door open, he was blasted with hot air and a haze of dust. The gate groaned and swung open heavily. He could see a tattered steel roof held up by rusting steel posts 200 feet ahead, and signaled to the Winemaker to drive on – he would walk. As the truck pulled forward, a huge billow of dust covered him from head to toe, blinding his eyes and causing him to choke.

His immediate reaction was to get mad, and then in a flash, he laughed at himself. I'm the king of dust, he thought, realizing his mistake and accepting the consequences of his actions. Sweat began to roll down his forehead, leaving muddy streaks across his cheeks, the sweat burning his eyes. Glancing over his shoulder he could just make out the field workers, slowly moving through the field. I guess some are in worse shape than me.

The Winemaker had already begun to unstrap the bins. He was wrapping up a long dusty strap into a nice neat roll. Joe grabbed the rest of the straps in a great heap and stuffed them into the truck. The Winemaker gave a glance of concern but didn't say anything. "Hey, we can stand in the heat and wrap them up now, or in the cool morning, don't you think Zen Master?"

"We will see, Grasshopper."

Within moments the trailer was unhitched and they were traveling back down the dusty trail. "Joe, jump out and close the gate."

"Okay boss." Back into the dust he went, but it didn't matter: he was one giant dust bowl from head to toe, with muddy streaks down his face looking like war paint. The Winemaker just laughed.

Joe washed up and changed into the next day's clothes in a gas station bathroom that was not much cleaner than he had been when he entered. Feeling clean and refreshed, he jumped into the truck with excitement. "Where we off to now?"

"Oh, I forgot to leave the grape order. You don't mind opening and closing the gate again do you?" the Winemaker said with a twinkle in his eye. Joe was exasperated, but quickly caught on to the joke when the Winemaker laughed, "In control huh?"

Foxen Canyon Road twisted and turned through fields, vineyards, scrub oaks, and horse farms, dotted with signs pointing every which way for local wineries. They traveled for about twenty-five miles up twisting backcountry roads, heading north into the Santa Maria Valley wine-growing region.

"I hope you don't mind Joe, but I want to check out this one vineyard for possibly next year's supply of Chardonnay. I know the grower. He's a wild guy, but he grows some fantastic fruit, and makes some exceptional wines."

After a few more twists and turns, they tucked into a small staging area adjacent to the vineyard. The place looked old and run-down. Rusty old equipment littered the area, but on closer inspection, it looked to be in working order.

Without a word, the Winemaker jumped out and started walking down a long row of vines, affectionately letting his hand brush against the leaves.

The vineyard was ablaze in gold and red hues, the leaves starting to wither and drop off. Mounds of rejected grapes, canes, and leaves littered the pathway. Small puffs of dust rose with every footfall, covering their boots. The fruit had been picked weeks earlier and the vineyard looked tired - as if it was ready to go to sleep for the winter.

"Over the winter, while the plant sleeps, the farmer will come through and prune the vines in preparation for next year." Row after row they walked, the Winemaker casually looking at the dormant vines as if in deep contemplation. "I love this time of year and walking the vineyards. I love the peace and tranquility and the beautiful display of color. Each vine is proud of what it accomplished. I could walk for hours meditating on the miracle of life and the bounty that Mother Nature has to offer."

They walked for another ten minutes, inspecting row after row. Joe finally asked, "What are you looking for? These plants look dead. Don't you want to see them when they have fruit and all?"

"To grow quality grapes requires three things: the right varietal, the right place, and the right person. We can get into details later, but for now, just realize that if you grow the right thing in the right place the right way, you will get quality. This applies to almost everything in life. You need these basic three qualities to become exceptional. Great wine starts in the vineyard.

"Louie, the grower, is a fascinating individual. I met him a few years ago when I spent an afternoon with him touring his vineyards. He is an old-timer, smart as a tack and with a memory like an encyclopedia. He owns thousands of acres of vines throughout Santa Barbara, and I swear he knows every vine. He spends most of his days walking the vineyards, checking on the vines with more intensity than a new father watches his baby. Point to any vine and he can tell you the clone, the rootstock, when it was planted, when it was grafted, and the awards it won. He can tell you the yield of each block for each year going way back into distant memory.

"Louie has a passion for his fruit, and it shows in his vineyard. I can't grow anything, and that's why I buy only from people who know how to grow fruit. Even though I can't grow, I can walk the vines and know when the grower is passionate about his craft. You can see it in the way it is designed, the way it is pruned. You can look at the dirt under the vines and the cover crop between the rows, and get a sense of what is going on.

"Santa Maria Valley is a natural funnel-shaped region that allows the cold Pacific winds to blow in off the ocean every night, cooling the area down dramatically. What grows best in this region is Pinot Noir and Chardonnay. Pinot Noir loves cold damp nights and foggy mornings and the Chardonnay will stay bright and refreshing with lemon and lime notes. Start with a good location and a good grower growing the right stuff, and what do you get Joe?"

"Quality fruit?"

"Are you growing the right stuff in the right location using the right way Joe?"

Joe paused. "I don't think so," he concluded, his head hung low.

The Winemaker smiled, and said, "First zen step is what? To see. And you see that you do not yet have these three principles mastered. That is okay. I firmly believe that one day, you will blossom with the most beautiful bounty, Grasshopper."

"Can we stop with the whole Grasshopper stuff?"

The Winemaker did not respond.

Leaving the vineyard behind, they traveled about fifteen miles south on the 101, taking an exit towards Los Alamos, a quintessential cowboy town of years long past. A broad Main Street cut through the heart of town, which was only two blocks wide. Stone and wood storefronts were adorned with weathered signs, which swung lazily in the hot afternoon air.

They pulled up outside of the 1880 Union Hotel, complete with a hitching post and a salon. "Ready for a frosty beer, Joe?"

"A beer? Don't winemakers drink wine?"

"On a hot day, filled with dust and weeks of processing fruit, I think a beer is a better choice."

After a few beers, burgers and hours, they decided to call it a night. "I'm staying at the motel across the street Joe. Where are you staying?"

Joe stood there dumbfounded. "I thought you made reservations for both of us," he stammered.

"Why would you think that Joe? You're a grown man, you have to take care of yourself."

There were no available rooms in town, and Joe was upset – not with the Winemaker, but with himself. He knew the

Winemaker had reinforced a critical lesson in life: you must be able to take care of yourself.

"Joe, there's a blanket behind the seat. It will keep you warm tonight. I have slept in the truck numerous times. Just consider it a life experience and lesson. Try to get some sleep. We are leaving for the vineyard at 3:30 in the morning."

The sun had set many hours before and the winds were cold. The seat was hard and the plastic was stiff. Joe shivered most of the night and was only able to catch brief snatches of sleep, always bolting upright as a car drove past, shivering and cursing under his breath.

At 3:33 Joe bolted out of a shallow slumber to see the Winemaker knocking on the frosted window. Billows of steam emerged out of his mouth as he told Joe to open the door. There was no moon, and the air was cold and still. The temperature had fallen to forty degrees and Joe was freezing. He stumbled out of the truck hugging himself and jumping up and down.

"What, no jacket Joe?"

CHAPTER 11

The new moon, no light, and the streets were silent as they drove to the vineyard. They turned off Baseline Road onto the gravel again. Eerie beams of artificial light shone ahead, lighting the staging area and casting everywhere else into pitch darkness.

Plumes of dust rose as tractors came and went, leaving with empty bins and returning with them filled with cold sleeping grapes. The rusty gate was open. As the truck turned the corner, the headlights flashed across the Koi Zen bins arranged in a long row, heaping to a perfect mound.

"Joe, we have a problem," the Winemaker said in a heavy tone. "Those bins are overfilled, well above my contracted weight."

Carefully he backed the truck up to re-hitch the now empty trailer, shaking his head with concern. The picking crew huddled around in the half-darkness, pointing to the bins and then the trailer, giggling and shaking their heads as they wondered if the trailer could carry the immense weight.

After a brief conversation with the forklift driver, one by one the bins were loaded onto the trailer. And with each bin, the trailer and truck squatted lower and lower, groaning and creaking in complaint. The Winemaker looked visibly worried. Joe decided that silence was the best option now, though his head was spinning with questions.

The bins were secured with many straps, each ratcheting down and tightening the load. The trailer strained under the immense weight of the cold fruit. The weight tags and delivery receipt were signed, and the two worried men climbed slowly into the cab.

"A few miles down the road is a gas station where we can fill up and check the straps to make sure our load is secure. It is always a very nervous time when heavy hauling, especially on these small country roads and on busy highways." With each bump, the truck and trailer complained. Their nerves were on high alert, and they were ready to respond to any indications of an issue. Creeping along well below the posted speed limit, the truck, crew, and cargo finally arrived at the gas station.

The gas station was small, so half the trailer remained in the road and the other half up the lot. This caused the axles to twist and turn, and made the wheels look like they would collapse any second.

"We are overloaded and I fear that we will have a hard time getting back to the winery in this condition. I have an idea though." The Winemaker made a quick call. "Hello Ian? Sorry to call you so early, but we just picked up a load of grapes and are severely overloaded. We need your help," he said as he was walking away. A few moments later he was heading back. "Okay, great. See you in about fifteen minutes. I owe you a big favor."

The pump clicked off and the trek began again, suspension groaning as the trailer twisted and turned in the small stormwater ditch next to the road. "The winery is about a half-mile away. My friend Ian is going to offload some fruit and ship it down for us. It always helps to have friends around you. You never know when you will be in a pinch."

As the trailer came around the corner, Ian stood in the parking lot laughing heartily. The Winemaker jumped out with a grin and gave his friend a firm handshake and a hug. "Thanks so much for getting out of bed and helping us out. As you can see, we are in bad shape right now."

"No problem, but you do owe me a beer – make that two beers."

"Done."

The trailer sighed in relief as two bins were swiftly plucked off with a forklift. Ian threw a cup of dry ice on each bin, and the whole stack was then wrapped in industrial-sized shrink wrap. A shipping sticker was slapped on the stack, and Ian said, "You should get this tomorrow morning. I'm glad I could help out. Safe travels friend." Within an hour the Winemaker and Joe were back on the road, feeling a little bit lighter, but still cautious of the long trip ahead of them.

Two hours passed in silence as they crept through Santa Barbara, still very attentive and on the lookout for any issues. As they approached Ventura, the traffic began to build, and so did the stress. Impatient cars continued to cut in front and around the heavily laden truck. Traffic remained heavy as they slowly made their way through Thousand Oaks and prepared for the heavy incline towards Calabasas.

Relegated to the truck lane, they climbed the Conejo Grade at twenty-five miles per hour, flashers on, and being passed by speeding cars and laboring trucks. They approached the summit and began to relax, giving Joe the perfect opportunity to ask a question that had been building in his mind.

"How can you remain so calm? This trip is obviously highly stressful, and yet it doesn't even seem to bother you at all. What is your secret?"

"Just continually practice being a Stoic. By understanding that neither I, nor you, can control how fast we travel, how the cars around us behave, and how heavy the traffic gets. All I can do is to make sure that I am staying safe, following the limitations around me and just keep going, mile by mile."

77

"Have you always been this calm?"

"In a previous life, I was a very different man than I am today. My life was filled with continual stress, conflict and bad choices that almost killed me."

"Killed you? How?"

"It's a long story that I will might share with you sometime. I was the sixteen-hour a day work guy, always chasing the dollar and the next big contract. I drank three pots of coffee and smoked a pack of cigarettes a day. I ate poorly and never exercised. My temper was short. It was a very dark time in my life – a time that I appreciate for the experience I had, the lessons I learned, but a place that I would never wish to go back to.

"I have found the winery has taught me to be a very different man. The stress is still there, just like this trip; however, it is a different type of stress. It is a stress that I have a small bit of control over. I can choose to drive or not. I can choose where I get my fruit from and how far I want to travel. I can choose when to pick the fruit and how. I can choose how to make the wine, which yeasts to use and what fermentation protocols to use. I can choose what type of barrels to use and how long to age the wine. I get to choose when to bottle and how long to let it bottle condition before I release it. Even with all the experience in the world, you are still not guaranteed that it will produce a good bottle of wine, which is stressful.

"After that, I lose much of the perceived control. I can't control if people like my wines, or if they come into the winery or what they buy. When it comes to these aspects, I am just a puppet.

"The old expression is, 'Making wine is easy, selling wine is hard.'"

"But all of your wines win gold and silver medals, you must be doing something right."

"All anyone can do is to always try their very best, with a clear head and heart. When we walked the vineyard yesterday, did you notice anything special about the place?" Joe shook his head, and the Winemaker continued, "Did you notice how dusty and bare the ground was, or how severely the vines were pruned? Did that seem odd to you?" Again, Joe shook his head no. "Grapes are very similar to people, Joe, and you can learn a lot from them. We talked about terroir and how the soil, the exposure, the local flora and fauna, the rain, the wind, and all the other local elements affect the grapes. However, there are two other parts that make a good bottle of wine. The first is the influence of the grower in the vineyard, and the second is the winemaker's influence.

"Often people neglect the influence of the grower, but they have a significant influence on the quality of the fruit. When we walked the vineyard, it was dusty and barren between the vines, and the cover crop was sparse. This vineyard lacked water and nutrients, which is a sign of a quality vineyard. The grower intentionally wants the fruit to struggle a bit, and to constantly be a little stressed. Doing this greatly increases the quality of the fruit.

"The reason is not as obvious as you think. A grape's sole mission in life is to try to procreate and spread its genes far and wide. Many people assume that grapes are ignorant, when in fact they are quite clever. For the fruit to procreate, it needs its seeds to be eaten by animals and spread far and wide. Each grape competes with every other grape, in terms of which will be eaten and which will not. Those that are not eaten, or picked, will drop to the ground, where there is little chance of surviving against its established parent.

"So, for a grape to survive, it wants to be eaten. When the farmer stresses the plant, the plant knows that it can't produce as much fruit as it desires, so it must be selective about how much to bloom and how many sprouts to grow. With fewer berries, the plant knows that to compete, it must produce the very best of the best fruit. So, by stressing the plant, the farmer can produce exceptional quality fruit.

"When the vines get too much water or nutrients, they get lazy and produce a great bounty of poor-quality fruit. Start with quality fruit and you get...?"

"A fighting chance to make a bottle of quality wine," Joe responded with a smug look.

"That's right. Now, this is where things get interesting. When we apply the same principles to people and businesses, we get the same results. Companies and managers often try to tempt employees to work harder by paying them more or giving them more perks. But what we find is just the opposite: people get lazy when they are not stressed. Just like grapes, the quality goes down and the problems go up. Now if the farmer or the manager creates too much stress, then things get bad very quickly. The quality drops, the plant dies and the employee quits. The moral of the story is twofold. First, one must realize that Mother Nature is very good at what she does, and one can learn a great deal about the way things work by mimicking her. Second, with just the right amount of stress, we get quality; with not enough or too much, we create problems.

"When a company is always pushing ahead, trying bigger and better things, or taking larger risks, the employees will almost always become inspired and rise to the challenge. When the company is flushed, it gets lazy, the employees get bored and even the most productive person will suffer. It's funny how that works, but it is true. However, as I said before, too much stress will also destroy a person or a company in a flash. This is what happened to me." The Winemaker fell silent, and Joe reflected on what he had said.

Joe hated his current job, not because it was too difficult – it was just boring. There were never any new challenges, or interesting assignments, just the same routine day after day. He had a yearning growing in his belly and was beginning to feel up to the challenge that would shortly come.

Ten hours after they had first set out with the sun setting, the truck rounded the last corner behind the winery. The Crush Crew let out a cheer and immediately got to work. Joe jumped out of the truck, excited at knowing what to do, and got busy. The Winemaker opened a beer leaning against the side of the truck and smiled, happy the long trip was complete and that everyone was safe.

Darius Miller

CHAPTER 12

Joe had a lot of time to think, with little to do at the office and the winery waiting for the last batch of grapes to finish fermentation.

He had discovered that by blocking out chunks of time, he could accomplish his duties at work in less than four hours. He set aside the first half-hour of his day to review all the critical tasks that needed to get done. These were put in a list from highest priority to lowest. Tasks that were important but not critical were placed on a second sheet. These would be accomplished when the critical list was empty.

For the next half-hour, he quickly reviewed his email – dragging high priority items to a "To-Do" folder. Low priority items were dragged to a "Later" folder. Everything else was either junked or unsubscribed; in less than a week, the number of emails and marketing pieces greatly diminished, making it easier to get through the email quickly.

For the next two hours, he turned off his phone and email and concentrated only on the high priority items, accomplishing them quickly and efficiently, since he was not often distracted. When a co-worker wanted to chat, he apologized and said they could meet up in the afternoon or at lunch.

When Larry popped in to micromanage him, he explained he was trying to be efficient and it worked best when he wasn't distracted. Larry soon backed off, giving Joe the freedom he needed for the afternoons.

By 11:00 he had made a major dent in his to-do items, feeling that he had accomplished more than he did in most days. He took a fifteen-minute break out of the office to clear his head.

Joe would sit in the small park across the street, or would walk a few blocks to grab a quick cup of tea at his favorite tea shop.

When he returned, most people were busy strolling around, chatting and waiting for their lunch break, but not Joe. He quickly responded to the most important email and wrapped up any loose ends. He had accomplished a complete day's work by lunchtime. While everyone was at lunch, Joe would meditate for half an hour. Then, when his peers were getting busy with the tasks they had ignored all morning, Joe was free to do whatever he wanted. His work was done, and now was the time to work on the most important project of all: himself.

He often thought about what the Winemaker had explained to him about 'seeing' reality, and used this as a newfound tool to analyze every situation. His meditations were beginning to allow him to reflect on and understand the random thoughts that coursed through his mind, especially when it came to emotions.

He began to understand what made him happy, or sad, or upset. He began to understand the triggers, and how to identify what set these triggers off. In the past, he would instantly become upset when conflict arose, but now he found himself saying, "Hey Joe, that thing that pisses you off just happened, how are you going to deal with it – like you always have, or is there a better way?"

This fleeting moment of reflection grounded him and soon he found that he was, if just a tiny bit, more in control of his mind than he had ever been.

In his mind's eye, he could imagine situations that made him happy, and analyze whether this was true happiness or just a 'grass-is-greener-on-the-other-side-of-the-fence' fantasy. What he thought most about was the winery and the people who frequented Koi Zen Cellars, and especially the friends he was making being part of the Crush Crew.

He found that each person was unique and came from a different place and background; however, they were all drawn to the same thing. Joe often wondered what that thing was. He had a feeling it would give him the answer to a question that he hadn't even asked yet, but one day would.

He also used the concept of 'swirling' and tried to explore new things and places. He intentionally tried new places to eat or new shops to explore, and new routes to go to the various places he went to. He was expanding, exploring, and it felt good to be out in the world instead of constantly being caught up inside of his head.

He began to understand the importance of mixing things up, to see the different sides of the situation and to seek alternate solutions and pose different questions. All these things made him feel more alive than he had in many years. He felt more in control of his thoughts and actions and was no longer someone else's puppet.

He quickly realized that the world was a very big place, filled with abundance. There was so much of everything waiting for him outside of these concrete walls. And he began to wonder why he had struggled to hold on to this small and meaningless job he had been coveting for so many years. He pondered the opportunities that his daughter Lucy would have, the places she would go and the things that she would do, and he desperately wanted to help make the world a better place for her and Mary. He wanted Mary to grow and to expand and blossom like the beautiful flower that she was – and his intimate relationship with Mary had also continuously improved.

The abundance all around him began to make him hungry to learn more, to explore more and – most importantly – to give more. He realized that for the last eight years he had been living in a shell, pushing this paper and pushing that paper all for someone else without meaning, without cause, and without passion. The only motivation was the almighty dollar, to buy things he didn't need or to spend money fixing things he didn't want.

The merger was getting closer and the tension in the office was very high, but Joe didn't feel the stress like his co-workers. Amongst this chaos, he was calm – eerily calm. He watched the drama unfold as if he was watching a movie in the theater. The actors were moving and the scenery was changing, but Joe wasn't in the movie, he was just watching it; enjoying some parts and disliking others. He was beginning to understand how to step out of the picture, contemplate his words before he spoke, and manage his emotions, allowing him to respond properly rather than constantly reacting.

All around him people talked in hushed whispers, always on edge. Managers' doors were often closed and upper management pointed at this and that while walking strangers through the office. Rumors came and went, but no one had a good idea of what was happening. Every time he asked Larry what was going on, he was brushed off, because even Larry didn't know what was happening most of the time. Indeed, Larry hadn't known what was going on for the last five years.

At 3:12, Joe's work had been done for three hours already and he was surfing the web. He started looking at job listings, and then click after click down the rabbit hole he went. He was watching surfing videos – funny how that happens – when Sally poked her head into his cubical.

"Hey Joe," the look of panic on her face could not be missed, "Uh, do you have a few moments... So, uh, we could chat?" she said, looking around her as if afraid she was being stalked.

"Sure Sally, what's on your mind?" Joe said, gesturing to a chair for her to sit down in.

"Uh, well, this is kind of," she hesitated, looking even more nervous, "something, um, personal. Can we take a break outside?"

Like two conspirators, the pair wove their path through the maze of cubicles and walked to the park, finding Joe's favorite bench empty.

Sally still looked very nervous and scared. "Joe I was walking back to my cube from the bathroom and was passing by Larry's office. Bill from Human Resources was in there, and it didn't look good. Larry had this blank stare on his face. He looked confused and panicked at the same time. All I heard was something about getting rid of our entire department!"

Joe didn't even flinch.

Darius Miller

CHAPTER 13

Sally was visibly upset and confused by Joe's reaction. In a hushed urgent tone, she said, "Joe, did you just hear what I said. They are going to close our entire department! All of us. We are all going to be fired! And you are just sitting there like a lump on a log. Don't you even care?"

"Sally, I know you are upset, but everything is going to be fine."

"Fine! How can it be fine when I'm out of a job! I'm going to lose my house, my car. I won't be able to pay my bills, and I'm going to end up living on the street, and you sit there and tell me it's going to be 'fine.' Do you know how long it took me to find this job? I'll never find a new one quick enough. Don't you get this, Joe?"

Calmly and compassionately Joe held up his hand to silence her. Then he said, "Sally, we will get through this just fine. Life is full of ups and downs, and for some, this is going to be a down. But for us, this is a blessing in disguise."

"How can you say that? We are going to lose our jobs. We won't have any money. It won't be fine. I don't know how you can say this. I'm freaking out right now, and you are just sitting there like some zen monk not giving a crap about anything."

"Oh Grasshopper, there is much to learn. What are you doing tonight?

"I want you to meet someone, someone I have come to respect. Someone who can help. Anyway, Mary is taking Lucy to a friend's house for a kid's play date and Sam is bowling tonight, right? So, I'll pick you up at 6:00. We are going to meet the Winemaker."

###

For a Tuesday night, there were a lot of cars in the winery parking lot and Joe had to park quite a distance from the entrance.

In confusion, Sally said, "I thought we were going to the winery?"

"We are. See the sign? Koi Zen Cellars."

"But where are the vineyards? We are in a business park in the middle of suburbia in Rancho Bernardo."

"Oh, Grasshopper" – Joe felt quite smug calling her Grasshopper – "growing grapes is farming. Making wine is manufacturing, and selling wine is retail. You don't go to the tomato farm to buy tomato sauce, do you? You go to the store. This is their store, tasting room, and manufacturing facility. Don't worry, you're going to love the place!"

The powerful aromas of fresh fruit, grapes and fermentation wafted out of the door as Sally pulled it open. "It smells wonderful!"

"Just you wait."

Frozen in the threshold, Sally couldn't believe her eyes. The whole winery was buzzing with activity. On the right were five or so tables, each covered in plastic and lined with women crafting away. Almost in unison, they all looked up, smiled and returned to their craft.

"Tonight, there is a mosaic tile class. They're making these mosaic trivets out of bits and pieces of broken ceramic tiles. At Koi Zen Cellars there is always some kind of community activity going on. I just don't know how Lisa, the Winemaker's wife, can coordinate all these activities. This place is all about building a strong community and helping people make the world a better place one glass at a time."

Each woman had piles of ceramic tiles, an instruction sheet and a trivet half-filled with glued-on titles. The pair wove their way through the maze of tables.

"This was the original tasting room and winery where the Winemaker and his wife Lisa first set up shop. This used to be Lisa's photography studio, and all the artwork on the walls is hers. After some kind of incident I don't know about, they decided to follow a dream and opened the winery. After two years, they were growing so fast that they were bursting at the seams. That is when the suite adjacent to them became available and they decided to expand," Joe said pointing through a double doorway and down two steps. "This side of the winery is still used for classes and special events like the mosaic class tonight. You can even rent out this entire side, or the other side for private events. Imagine how cool it would be to have your own private party in a winery! I've just booked my birthday party here in a few months. Want to come?

"Anyway, they were growing so fast that they had to expand both the tasting rooms and the production space. Back there," Joe said, pointing to a double door at the end of the bar, "was the original production space. Now it's filled with barrels of aging wine and cases of wine ready for sale. The real action happens on the other side. Let's go see it."

They turned to the left and stepped down two steps. "On the left is the Zen Room. This is a great place to meet a friend or read a book. Do you see the circular doorway? That was inspired by a trip to China when they visited a place called Lingering Gardens. The whole winery is very zen-like; very calming and relaxing, but also very lively at times, like tonight."

On the lower level, people were sitting on high-top chairs around glass-covered barrels, sitting at small square tables, relaxing on comfortable couches or chairs, or bellied up to the long marble bar. Each with a glass of wine, looking up, smiling and then getting back to their personal conversations.

"The expansion allowed them to create different areas where people can cluster and hang out. And through those doors is the newly expanded production area. That's probably where we'll find the Winemaker."

The lower tasting room was full of people, but not overly crowded. Everyone looked to be having a great time, with clusters of people here and there laughing or talking, some on their phones or taking pictures, and some talking to each other the old-fashioned way.

They navigated to the end of the room and Joe slid open two large barn doors. The contrast between the tasting room and the production area was remarkable. While the tasting room was calm and relaxing, filled with soft muted earth tones, the production area was filled with shiny stainless-steel tanks, wooden barrels, white walls, and long LED strip lights. Sally didn't know what to make of the space. After the living room feel of the tasting room, it looked like an automobile manufacturing plant.

The walls were lined with barrels, each stacked to the ceiling four high. On the back right were large stainless-steel tanks that reached towards the sixteen-foot high ceiling and smaller steel tanks between them. In the center of the room were two rows of white plastic bins covered in plastic. The Winemaker was at the far end, standing on a bench mixing the grapes with a long stainless-steel paddle.

The Winemaker looked up and said, "Hey Joe, great to see you. You must be the doctor?"

Sally looked confused. "I'm not a doctor."

"Then how are you going to cure cancer? I might be mistaken, but I thought that's what Joe said you wanted to be."

Sally stood in the doorway between these two realities, not sure what to say, do, or even how to respond, so she remained quiet.

"Yeah, he can be a little intense," Joe said in a hushed tone.

"Come on over Sally, so that I can properly meet you. Oh, on the way, sanitize your hands. You don't mind a little work do you Sally?"

Joe just giggled to himself – he knew what was in store for her. Joe pointed to a bucket filled with what appeared to be water and instructed Sally how to properly wash her hands and arms. "Sally, anything that touches grapes either directly or indirectly must be sanitized. This solution will help kill any of the buggies that can spoil the wine. Keeping clean is the most important rule around here."

Sally squatted down and began cleaning her hands and arms as instructed. She then grabbed the bin and pulled herself up. "Sorry, Sally, you just contaminated yourself by touching the bin. Try again." A little frustrated, but understanding, she scrubbed again and stood up without assistance.

"Ok, come on over guys. We are punching down the Cabernet Franc that Joe and I picked up a few days ago from Santa Ynez Valley."

Sally looked devilishly at Joe. "Stomach flu?"

Joe just hung his head sheepishly, knowing he had been caught in a fib.

"Sally, I hear that you are a little freaked out right now. Maybe I can help, maybe not. But what I do know is that some good old-fashioned physical labor can often help." He quickly showed Sally how to punch down the grape bins. Joe just stood to the side smiling. The Winemaker stepped down and watched Sally struggle with the tool. "Another student to do your work, Zen Master?" Both men smiled watching Sally slowly forcing the paddle through the cap.

###

"Sally, there are over 14,000 pounds of grapes in these bins. We as winemakers and winemaking students need to help Mother Nature along during fermentation. We can't directly control fermentation; all we can do is assist it and make sure it happens the right way.

"The sunlight falls on the leaves of the vines. The vines convert the sunlight to energy to grow and produce fruit. This is all about survival and, more importantly, procreation. When the baby grapes emerge, they are extremely bitter and nothing wants to eat them. This is how immature seeds protect themselves from being eaten. As the summer heat builds, the acids in the grapes begin to fall and the berries begin to grow larger. The sugar content also starts to increase, to make the berries more attractive to the animals. The berries are still green in color and are camouflaged by the leaves until about June or July when the red grapes begin to change color. Farmers call this the veraison. For red varietals, the green grapes transform into darker colors of red, purple and even almost black. This signals to the animals that the fruit is getting sweet but is not quite ready. Depending on the varietal and the location, the fruit will be fully ripe about six weeks later. During this last phase, the berries become much larger, sweeter, less acidic and darker.

"At optimal ripeness, the fruit is picked and immediately processed into wine. Oh, Sally, don't forget the corners."

Sally looked up with a look half of disdain and half of amusement.

"But that isn't the end of the transformation. Once the fruit arrives at the winery, we first remove the bitter-tasting stems and prepare the berries for fermentation. We add yeast, and the yeast converts the sugars to alcohol. That is what is happening right now. Every few hours we must mix the grapes to keep everything wet, consistent and to introduce oxygen into the fermenting grapes. After about two weeks the sugar is gone and all the alcohol has been produced. The liquid is now wine and will age in barrels for many months.

"So, we start with a seed, which grows a vine, which produces a grape, which is turned into wine, which is then bottled, drunk and eliminated. Quite a bit of change, huh?"

As Sally had been laboring punching down the grapes, she was captivated by the process the Winemaker laid out. She knew there was a subtle message in there, but she was a little unsure how it related to their company restructuring, and she and Joe losing their jobs. Within moments small beads of sweat appeared on her brow as she labored to push the paddle through the thick cap of grape skins and force them down into the juice below.

With every push, the juice foamed and frothed around the tool, releasing warm puffs of deep, complex, intoxicating aromas. The air was mixed with the smells of sweet fruit, alcohol, deep earth smells, green notes of bell pepper, fresh-cut grass and bready yeast. The more she pushed and punched, the deeper into a hypnotic rhythm she sank. The worries of the day began to melt away and a serene calmness came over her. The more she sweated, the calmer she became. Glancing up, she saw Joe and the Winemaker leaning against other bins filled with fermenting fruit.

"Feels good to work up a sweat doesn't it?" the Winemaker asked.

"I haven't worked out this hard in years. It feels great – and smells delicious also."

With a smirk, Joe said, "Glad you are having a good time. Only six more bins to go," remembering his first experience punching down.

And just as Joe had experienced, soon Sally was covered in the sweet sticky juice of the wine, staining her hands and clothes. But for the first time in a long time, she felt accomplished and content. She could see her direct efforts were making a change, and that she was doing it. She was making things happen, and it felt good.

A few moments later, she moved the stepstool to a new bin and began punching down again, remembering to sanitize her arms and hands since she had touched the bench and bins. The Winemaker smiled.

When Sally began to show signs of struggle on the third bin, Joe offered to take over, which was greatly appreciated. Sally hadn't done that much physical labor in twenty years, but beneath the fatigue was a great sense of actual accomplishment.

"Come on Doc," the Winemaker said, "after all that hard work, how about a sip of wine and we can chat about the real reason Joe brought you here tonight while he finishes up?"

"I don't know why you keep calling me a doctor. I'm not a doctor – I just wanted to get my Ph.D. so I could do cancer research."

"I'm confused. If that is what you want to do, then why are you working with Joe and not in a laboratory?"

"I don't know. I met Sam, my husband, in graduate school and we got married, we bought a house and settled down. That's what married people do. I found a job where Joe works five years ago, and I guess I just gave up on my dream."

"So, you must really like your job then?" the Winemaker probed.

"No, but it pays the bills – well, I hope it does. There's a good chance that both Joe and I are going to get laid off, and it scares me."

"Why? Because you like your job?"

She shook her head no.

"Because you like the company?"

Again, she responded no.

"Do you like your boss and don't want to let them down?"
Still no.

"Because you are going to find your dreams fulfilled in your current job?"

No again.

"So, let me get this straight: you are scared of losing something that you don't like, does not inspire you, does not offer stability and is causing you to not follow your dream."

She nodded yes.

Just then Joe came around the corner breathing heavily, glistening beads of sweat across his brow, to hear the summation.

"Well Joe, what do you think she needs to do?"

Both men simultaneously said, "Empty your cup!"

"Empty my cup? But you just filled it with wine."

"No, silly," Joe said. "He means your mind."

"Sally," the Winemaker started softly, "often people do the same thing over and over. They go to the same places, do the same things. It becomes a habit, a routine, and it feels safe. Now people like to feel safe, so what we do is, we start to build walls on either side of our path. These walls feel safe and secure. We build these walls brick by brick by telling ourselves that the known is much better than the scary new things out there. We rationalize all kinds of reasons for not changing, and that it is better to stay the same and not change. But just like sandpaper on wood, it wears you down, day by day and bit by bit, and every day we build the walls higher and higher. We dig a deep rut, and the deeper the rut, the harder it is to climb out.

"Remember we talked about how sunshine causes the vines to produce fruit, and after many changes, it finally becomes the nectar of the gods? If these changes did not happen, then we would never be able to share a glass of wine together. There is

97

only one thing that never changes. Do you know what that is Sally?"

Mesmerized, she shook her head no.

"The thing that never changes is change itself. Change will always happen, and once you realize that nothing is permanent, then suddenly you appreciate the preciousness of each moment, experience or opportunity. Does that make sense to you?"

"Yes, but I need that job to pay the...." She cut herself off, seeing that the Winemaker wasn't going to buy her story no matter how passionately she told it.

"That is your old story. I can see that your mind is full of all kinds of walls, chains, restrictions, and worries. For an opportunity to find its way in, you must make space for it. You need to create a wide-open space so that no matter where it lands, you will catch it. The only way to do that is to empty your mind. Think of your mind like an old attic. All the stuff that you do not use, but for some reason want to keep, goes up into the attic. It stays there neglected and forgotten, collecting dust, serving no purpose other than to take up space. Every time you think that you should clean the attic, you look around, and there is so much stuff and the task appears so daunting, and so what do you do? You turn off the light and go back downstairs.

"Now some people become attached to all of the stuff in the attic and can't bear to part with it. They remember the time when they got that junk and reminisce on days gone by. They live in the past, often desiring to return to a place that no longer exists. Time has moved on, but they have not. They believe all their stuff makes them feel a sense of accomplishment, when it is actually just clutter causing them to feel unhappy and remorseful.

"Sally, is your attic filled with junk that is holding you back?"

Tears filled her eyes and she nodded yes.

"Do you want to change? Do you want to move on and become the person you want to be?"

She nodded, her expression indicating excitement and anticipation.

"Well you can Sally; you just need to take a step in the direction of your dreams and passions. Just take that one little step."

###

Early the next morning, Sally was almost bouncing off the walls as she rushed into Joe's cube, grabbed him by the arm and dragged him outside. Her smile could light up the world and she had a childish giddiness to her. In a conspiratorial whisper, she said, "Last night after I left the winery my head was spinning. Sam had gone to bed early, since he had to get up very early today to catch a plane. So, I sat in the dark, just thinking. And I began to imagine a new future, one in which I was a doctor and helping to cure cancer. Every time something negative popped into my head, I just said, 'Junk' and imagined a huge dumpster in the corner of my attic and threw that thought away. I must have sat there in the dark for four hours, and then I had a thought.

"I remembered that my old roommate in grad school worked locally at a cancer research center here in San Diego. I haven't thought about her for five years now, but I grabbed my phone and texted her, telling her that I wanted to catch up. Well, thirty seconds later she called me. It was the middle of the night but she called me anyway. We talked for over an hour.

"And do you know what? She is a principle partner in this small cancer research company. When I explained my big dream, she told me that they had a lab tech position open and that I could have the job if I wanted. She offered me a job right there on the spot! During grad school, we were very close. We both knew how hard the other worked, and how well we worked together. Anyway, the lab tech position is kind of a junior position, but it pays a little more than I make here. But you know the best part?" She looked at Joe, who now was also smiling, but he shook his head no. "They will pay for my Ph.D. program! In two years and eight months, I will be Dr. Sally McAlister! Thanks for all of your help! I have to run - meeting in 5 minutes." She bounded off, almost skipping away, while Joe remained on the bench.

He sat there smiling quietly, and something very deep stirred within him. For the first time in a long time, he felt truly happy for someone else's good fortune. It was a strange feeling, like being a proud father. It was a feeling that would soon drive him in a new direction.

Joe looked at the people milling around the park, the bright sky with wisps of clouds, the red and brown leaves blowing in the wind. Even though he was no closer to solving his situation, he said out loud to the squirrel that was running away with an acorn in its mouth, "It's a good day."

CHAPTER 14

Joe was packing up his lunch box and briefcase. Frank was standing in the doorway of his cube, gossiping about office politics that Joe didn't care about. At 4:15, Joe got a text message: "Wine blending trials tonight @ 6:30."

"Hey Frank, you're a wine snob, right?"

Frank nodded, amused.

"Well, do you want to blend some wine with me tonight at the winery?"

Frank was going through a horrible divorce and hated going back to the hotel each night. He agreed immediately. Together they left a "little" early and grabbed a bite to eat at a burger joint.

Sitting around two pints of beer chomping on their burgers, Joe began to explain his experiences at Koi Zen Cellars and with the Winemaker. Joe confessed about his mystery stomach bug.

Frank laughed and laughed.

"Why are you laughing about me faking a stomach bug?"

"Come on Joe, do you think anyone bought that story? The whole office knew you were faking it."

"Well, Larry bought it!"

Frank almost choked on his beer, foam dripping out of the corners of his mouth and his eyes tearing up. "Now that's funny! So where is this winery of yours, up in the hills?"

"No, it's right down the street, about a quarter-mile."

"But there aren't any vineyards on World Trade Drive. I drive that road all the time, going back and forth from the fitness center."

"Didn't you ever see the big purple flags next to the road that says 'Wine Tasting' and 'Open' flapping in the breeze?"

"I guess not."

"Well, I suggest you start looking around, buddy. A lot of stuff is going on around the office, and I don't want any of you guys getting blindsided."

Joe spent the next twenty minutes explaining the concept of a craft winery. "You see Frank, growing grapes is farming, making wine is manufacturing. You don't have to make the wine where it is grown. There are so many advantages of not owning vineyards.

"As a craft winery, the Winemaker can choose grapes from anywhere he wants. Some grapes grow better in Santa Barbara, or Santa Maria, or Sonoma or Napa. He gets to choose only the finest fruit from where it grows the best and brings it here to make the wine. I've been helping him, hence the 'stomach bug' that seems to come and go.

"If you own the land, then you are stuck with the fruit that it produces. Some places grow great grapes, and other places the grapes are crap, and it varies from vineyard to vineyard and even row by row. If you own it, you are stuck with it. Now the farmers have it rough. They take all the risk. If the fruit has an issue like mold, or mildew or birds, animals, frost, hail, rain, or myriad other things, then the farmer loses. But the Winemaker has a quality clause in all his contracts. He doesn't have to accept damaged fruit, and if the grapes from the farmers he has contracts with are damaged, he can always go to another vineyard to source the fruit."

"But how does he know which fruit is good and which is bad? Does he go up and taste the fruit before he buys it?"

"He can, but most of the time he will check out the vineyards the year before and find out who is making wine from that fruit and check it out. When I went up to pick up the Cabernet Franc—"

"You mean when you were out sick?"

"Yeah, as I was saying, we went to check out a new vineyard for next year. When we walked the vineyard, you could tell that the farmer cared about his fruit. That's a good sign of the quality of the fruit. The more passion someone has about something, usually the better it is. The Winemaker jokes about trying to find the farmer who sings the grapes lullabies and wipes the early morning dew off each berry."

The Winemaker was sitting at a large oak table with four people Joe didn't know. The table was covered with unlabeled bottles of wine, glass beakers, pipettes, dump buckets, blank sheets of paper, and pens. The Winemaker glanced up as they opened the door. "Welcome Joe, who's your friend?"

"Oh, wise Zen Master Winemaker," Joe said. "This is Frank. He works with me. He's a wine expert."

"An expert!? Wonderful. Welcome to Koi Zen Cellars, Frank. Pull up a chair and I will explain how this whole thing is going to work."

Everyone first introduced themselves and then leaned forward in excited anticipation of the night's activities.

"Even though we are still finishing up the harvest, it is never too early to start thinking about next year's wines. Tonight, I want to see if we can develop a Left Bank style blend to released next year, late spring."

Everyone nodded, except for Frank, who was a little confused by the Left Bank comment. Catching Frank's reaction and without missing a beat, the Winemaker continued, "In the Bordeaux region in France, there are two primary regions. The Left Bank produces Cabernet Sauvignon-based wine blends, and the Right Bank produces Merlot-based blends. Tonight, we are looking to develop a Cabernet Sauvignon-based blend.

"Now in the Bordeaux region of France they grow five primary red grape varietals, does anyone know what they are?"

Almost in unison, except for Frank, the choir responded, "Cabernet Sauvignon, Merlot, Cabernet Franc, Malbec, and Petite Verdot."

The Winemaker smiled and nodded in approval.

"Our job tonight is to try to develop a blend that has structure, interest, and complexity."

As he said this, Frank perked up. Frank had always dreamed of being an architect, and these words resonated with him. A building needed to look nice, it had to be functional, it needed to be interesting and to have a certain look that made people say, "Wow!"

The Winemaker saw Frank's reaction and asked, "Designer?"

Frank shook his head and responded, "Architect."

"Close enough," the Winemaker said with a smile.

"We are going to evaluate each of the base wines for color, body, acids, tannins, flavors, attack, finish, sugar and alcohol. In front of each of you are evaluation sheets for each wine. We will be tasting each wine, going from the lightest body and tannic structure to the heaviest. There are breadsticks to cleanse your palate and a spit bucket – I don't want anyone consuming too much tonight."

Liz asked, "Could you explain why we are blending? Aren't wine blends junky wines, you know, like table wines?"

"A lot of people think the same thing Liz, but some of the most expensive wines, such as a Left Bank Bordeaux, are blends. By blending we can create something magical. You see, each wine has a unique and distinct set of qualities to it. Some wines are aromatic, some are fruit-forward, some have a long finish, etcetera. By blending these together, we can create a wine that has the best qualities of each of the individual wines put together. Suppose we want more color in the wine. Blending a little Petite Verdot will achieve this, but will also add a lot of tannins. So, there are always tradeoffs with blending. In general, the Cab Sauv will bring body and character. The Merlot brings a soft fruitiness. Malbec brings an earth element and the Cabernet Franc brings a light green element.

"Some of the wines will be fruit-forward, some support the middle, and others have a long finish. Our goal is to develop a balanced blend, that has a solid beginning, middle, and long finish, with a good balance of acidity, tannins and a smooth silky alcohol body. Okay, let's get started. Please record your trials and share with others, and please don't swallow too much. It dulls the taste buds and senses, so please spit your wine."

Everyone grabbed a couple of evaluation sheets, a pen and a bunch of blending glasses. Concoctions were created, evaluated and tossed. Frank got into blending the wine. In his mind's eye, he was creating a beautiful structure. It needed to be interesting and complex, while remaining light and beautiful. His design skills were aching to be exercised after working for so long in insurance. With each new blend, he became more excited and determined to find the perfect combination.

"So Frank, during high school I thought about being an architect also. Do you enjoy it?" asked the Winemaker.

"Oh, I'm not an architect. I work with Joe at the insurance company."

"Then why did you tell me you were an architect?"

"I guess inside I've always wanted to be an architect, it just didn't work out that way."

"Frank, we only ride this merry-go-round called life once, and you need to follow your passions and fulfill your true destiny. So, why aren't you an architect, if that is what you always wanted to be?" Frank couldn't find an answer and felt a little hollow inside. He didn't know why, and deep down it made him feel a little humiliated and sad. To run from his pain, he got even busier blending wines.

As he began to understand what was happening while he adjusted the ratios of the different wines, the image of an ideal wine began to form in his mind. Just like designing a building, each part of the architecture contributed to the whole. Too much of this and it became unbalanced, too little of that felt weak and uninspiring, like a drab gray building. The more he blended, the more engrossed he became – and the further away slipped the problems of his life, his work, and his lack of dreams.

The blending continued for two hours until the group started to hone in on the final blend. Not listening to the Winemaker, Frank refused to spit, claiming he couldn't properly evaluate the wine without swallowing. He was now obviously drunk.

"Joe, your friend is cut off. I hope he has a safe ride home because no matter how expensive or inconvenient it is, driving tipsy is not an option."

Joe, who also hadn't been spitting as much as he should, threw his keys on the table and with a slight slur said, "We will rideshare home."

"Good choice Joe, your car will be safe in the parking lot overnight. And I am glad that you have the common sense to know your limits. I'm very impressed Joe."

The words of appreciation and acknowledgment filled his heart with a wonderful feeling. He seldom felt needed and worthy, but he was beginning to change. It was truly a good day.

The night air was cold as Joe and Frank stood in the parking lot waiting for their ride. Joe was rubbing his arms trying to warm up, but Frank just stood there, impassive and unmoving.

"Are you okay Frank?"

With sadness in his eyes, Frank turned to Joe and said, "I want to be an architect. I'm done with insurance."

Their ride appeared and the two men were driven safely home.

###

Mary had an early morning doctor's appointment. There wasn't enough time to pick up Joe's abandoned car from the previous evening's activities, so she drove him directly to work and would drive him over to the winery during his lunch break after her appointment. The fall morning was bright and crisp, and being in the passenger seat allowed Joe to really look around and enjoy the scenery.

The leaves had all changed into their fall colors. The array of red, orange and yellow leaves contrasted against the tall palm trees swaying in the morning breeze. Mother Nature was signaling change, and he knew that soon there would be change at the office for him. However, he just felt adrift, not knowing where he was headed and how he would respond to the changing work conditions – if he even had a job.

As usual, he plowed through his work in record time by staying focused and blocking out time to accomplish tasks without interruption. His phone beeped just before noon; it was a message from Mary saying she was waiting for him outside. He packed up his belongings and shut down his computer. It was going to be another short workday, but he had finished all his daily duties and could take a few hours off. He could see Mary's radiant smile as he approached the car.

Acting like an excited schoolgirl, Mary said, "Guess what?"

"Oh, I don't know – you're happy to see me?"

"No silly, but you're close. Do you want to see an ultrasound of your new baby boy!"

"A boy! Mary that's wonderful! Is everything okay? I didn't know you were having an ultrasound!"

"Everything is doing just fine. No issues and he is definitely a boy! The doctor just thought I was a little big and wanted to make sure I wasn't having twins."

"That's my boy! Want to grab some lunch and celebrate?"

"Sorry, but Lucy is with Peggy and I am meeting them at the library for storytime. Want to come with us?"

"Nah, I have to get my head screwed on straight about this whole job thing. I'm going to go sit in the park and meditate for a few hours. Is that okay?"

"Of course it is," she said as the pulled into the winery parking lot, "Just don't drink too much while you are meditating," she joked. Joe blushed.

He had only planned on popping into the winery to say hi, but Annie was giving a private wine tasting, which piqued his interest. Quietly, he grabbed a glass of water and sat with his back to the group, far enough away so as not to appear to be listening, but close enough to hear everything said."

"Okay guys, what is the first zen step of wine tasting?"

The group in unison said, "Seeing."

"And the second zen step of wine tasting is…?"

Everyone excitedly said, "Swirling."

Joe smiled, thinking about how these little steps had begun to change his life.

"Now the third zen step of wine tasting is to 'smell.' Now we are going to perform a little experiment that you will find very interesting, but I need everyone's cooperation. Got it?" Everyone nodded in approval. Annie was so good at captivating the group. Everyone was having a good time, and she was an expert teacher and entertainer. She was also one of the two sommeliers that were on staff at Koi Zen Cellars.

"Now, this is the important part: do not touch your glass after I pour the wine, got it?"

In bated anticipation, everyone agreed, not knowing what was going to happen next. Joe quickly went to the second bar and asked for a small tasting of the Cabernet Franc.

He got back to his little table just as Annie finished pouring the last sample. The anticipation of the group was palpable. Annie proceeded, "Our next sample is a Cabernet Franc from Santa Ynez Valley. We are honored and humbled by the fact that this wine has won two gold medals in international competitions and a double gold in another competition." Now the group was very engaged and hung on every word she said. Being a performer, she played the crowd and they loved it.

"At Koi Zen Cellars we are all about being mindful and present in each and every moment." The words hung in the air, everyone attentive and focused. "So we approach wine tasting in the same manner. So many people are wrapped up living in the past or are projecting fantasies of the future, but this moment is the only moment that truly exists. So, everyone, take a couple of deep breaths and get ready to be mindful." Everyone, including Joe and Annie, took a few deep breaths and became centered.

"Smell is one of the oldest sensory organs. Through smell, animals could detect dangerous plants, predator scents, or when a female was in heat. Smell was and is very important to animals. Have you ever watched a dog 'smell the pee-mail'?" Everyone chuckled, including Joe, who was caught red-handed listening to the conversation. Annie smiled and continued,

"However, most of us now live in a very sterile environment where we don't encounter dangerous scents except for things like spoilage and smoke. Other than that, we don't use our noses that often, and smell has become a lost art.

"The good news is that everyone can learn how to improve their nose quite easily, and we will get to that in a moment. So, everyone, slowly pick up your glass as still as possible and take a couple of quick whiffs." Joe and the rest of the group did so and Annie continued her presentation, "What you are picking up are the lightest aromas. These tend to be floral and perfume smells. The smells of spoilage are often the lights aromas also.

"Wine is a living colony of microscopic organisms; some are good and some are rather stinky. In the winery, we need to be very clean when we make the wine so that we can keep the good organisms and keep the bad ones away. One of the most common smells of a spoiled wine is caused by a spoilage organism called Brettanomyces, or Bret for short. This little guy can have a whole host of funky aromas such as manure, barnyard, cat pee, nail polish remover, wet horse, etc." Now everyone had a look of disdain. "It may not smell great, but it won't hurt you, and some people like those smells." This elicited a round of confused looks and people shaking their heads in disagreement.

"Another common wine fault is caused by the buildup of hydrogen sulfide, which smells like rotten eggs or sewer." There was another round of unhappy faces. "But you really won't find those smells in our wines. The reason is that we stay—"

Joe blurted out, "CLEAN!"

Everyone laughed.

Joe sheepishly lowered his head, pretending that outburst had not happened.

Annie continued, "So smell your wine again and tell me what you smell."

"I smell green peppers, no – wait – jalapenos," one lady said.

Everyone sniffed again, and almost everyone agreed.

"Also a bit of floral and spice, but I can't identify it," she continued.

"Great. Now what I would like you to do is give your glass a big swirl and smell again."

Joe did so and was amazed at the difference. The wine completely changed characteristics. The jalapenos, floral and spice were still there, but more pronounced, and the smell of red fruit, raspberry, and strawberry had emerged. Expressions of surprise and wonder appeared on the faces around the bar, and the guests continued to swirl and sniff, all agreeing on their collective assessment of the smells.

"Now are you ready for a really geeky thing?" Annie asked with a devilish look in her eye. "Gently put your hand over the opening of your glass and swirl. We want to trap all those aromas inside of the glass. Go ahead, give it a good swirl, and quickly smell your glass."

Again, the characteristics of the wine changed dramatically. Now Joe could smell deep rich elements, like a touch of damp earth, tobacco, and gravel. He looked at his glass in amazement at how, by paying attention to what you are doing, really being in the moment, aware of what you are doing, could make such a huge difference. He had had this wine many times before, but this was the first time he began to understand its nuances and subtle tastes. There has to be a lesson in this – there always is a lesson at the winery, he thought. He quietly got up from his chair and headed to the park deep in thought.

How is it that the smell of the wine could change so much by not swirling, swirling and then covering and swirling? he wondered, sitting on a rock under the shade of a large Torrey

Pine tree near the edge of the pond. He watched the small fish moving in unison without communicating. He watched the turtles pop their heads out to catch a breath before slowly descending to the depths. The trees swayed and people walked along the path, most of them unfortunately engrossed in their phones and not on the beauty surrounding them.

The more he thought about his recent experience, the more his mind drifted to the office. Was he 'seeing' what was really going on, or was he wandering around not mindful of the situation? Was he 'swirling' to see all the different aspects, or was he on autopilot doing the same thing repeatedly? And was he 'smelling' the surroundings, looking for and identifying all those things around the office, and his life, that didn't quite smell right, like smoke in the distance?

He thought of the company refrigerator where he found a container of his with some mystery food in it a few days ago. What had he done? He'd cautiously opened the lid and looked at it, trying to decide if it was worth eating or completely spoiled. Then he smelled it, trying to detect that aroma of spoilage. It was spoiled, and he didn't dare 'swirl' it in fear of making a huge mess. It quietly went directly into the trashcan, container and all.

But what else was going on in his environment that he wasn't paying attention to? The downside of being so task-focused at the office was that he wasn't having the water cooler talks he used to, and was becoming very disengaged from his colleagues. Then he thought about something even more profound: the things going on inside of him that he wasn't paying attention to.

He thought about the gym membership he never used. Or the massage appointments that were missed, or the lack of spending quality time with Mary and away from Lucy. He knew that his self-care regimen needed some serious work, and with that, he briskly walked around the lake for the next thirty minutes before returning home to help Mary cook dinner.

Even as Joe pulled into the driveway, he could hear the loud music and singing emanating out of his house. The music was blaring and Mary was singing, "The wheels on the bus go round and round..."

Lucy was in her high chair, swinging her legs and squealing in delight as Mary was prepping dinner.

Joe just smiled at the energy in the room. "Having fun?" he yelled above the loud children's song.

It took Mary a moment to realize that Joe was home. She turned down the children's song, much to Lucy's dismay. She was radiant with energy and bubbling all over. "Joe, the most incredible thing happened today!" Joe grabbed a beer from the fridge and sat down next to Lucy, kissing her on the forehead. She was still banging spoons on the edge of her chair.

"Joe, I am so excited about knowing that we are having a baby boy! Now Lucy will have a younger brother to beat up on but who will always defend her. The perfect match. But that isn't all of the good news. Lucy and I went to the library for storytime, but the storyteller never showed up. When I tried to explain this to Lucy, she burst into tears, which crushed me. In a pinch, I grabbed a random book off the shelf and sat on the floor and started to read. Lucy immediately sat down, and within a few moments another young boy sat down. Then another and another. I felt like the Pied Piper. With every sentence, more and more kids sat down, forming a circle around me. Each one was glued to every word, and there wasn't a single peep out of the whole bunch.

"I finished the story, and then the kids wanted one more, which led to one more and so on. They were really into it and I felt like a performer. It was great. But the best part was that after six books, an older lady approached me and told me, 'You are a wonderful teacher, thank you!' I was dumbfounded, I'm not a teacher but it felt so good to read stories to those kids. I know it doesn't mean much in the big picture, but that moment was so very special to me. Entertaining and educating those young minds was miraculous."

"Mary, you are so good with Lucy, how could you not be with the other children? Are you still considering becoming a teacher?"

"Joe, get real. I'm going to be a mom of two kids and you are talking about being a teacher?"

"Yeah, why not? You are a natural, you have to admit that!"

Sheepishly she said, "Well, the librarian thought I did a good job also. She told me that their current volunteer for Sunday book reading couldn't make it for the next two months and offered it to me. Me, simple humble me, is now an official storyteller. But do you know what? The idea of being a teacher kind of appeals to me. I know it is a thankless job, but it just feels right to me."

Something clicked inside of Joe. He didn't know what it was, but it was closer – closer to what, he didn't have a clue, but it felt good, whatever it was.

CHAPTER 15

The Cabernet Franc grapes that Joe had helped pick up were getting close to the end of the fermentation and he was excited to taste the almost finished baby wine. He had been tracking its progress every time he visited the winery, and tonight was no different.

The parking lot was crowded even though most of the businesses were closed. He found a spot and enjoyed the brief walk to the winery in the cool autumn evening. Crickets jumped around the sidewalk and he was careful to watch where he stepped – he didn't want to bring any bad karma to the winery.

The winery was packed. The weekly live music always drew a crowd and this band, Riptide, packed the house every time. The band was just setting up and the energy was high and felt very festive. Joe first looked in the production area for the Winemaker, but he wasn't there. Then he checked the old production area, now filled with large stacks of case goods and barrels, but again he wasn't there. Joe had seen the Winemaker's old sports car in the parking lot, but couldn't find him.

The staff pointed to the office. Joe knocked on the office door, then slowly opened it and peeked in. The Winemaker was sitting in the office chair, head down and tears running down his face.

"Are you okay?" he asked tentatively.

The Winemaker straightened up and wiped the tears from the corners of his eyes. He looked upset, and Joe was compelled to assist the man who had helped him so much. Seeing Joe's questioning eyes, the Winemaker said, "Sorry, sometimes something triggers some dark memories of the past that I still have a hard time dealing with."

Joe was shocked: the man who always seemed to have a calm and calculated response was deeply human. There was a full case of wine sitting on the floor, and Joe sat down without saying a word, but the message was clear: "I'm here if you need to talk."

The Winemaker wiped the remaining tears away, then turned to Joe and said, "Sorry about that. I was reading the news, which I very rarely do – don't worry about what you can't control – and read about the tsunami that hit the southern Philippines. A thousand dead and twice that missing. Ten times that displaced or have lost everything. Mother Nature can be a bitch when she wants to be, and all this death and destruction plays heavily on my heart. It also brings back bad memories from a past life, a past that I am not very proud of – though I think of it often."

Joe's mind was filled with questions about this elusive past the Winemaker hinted about but never spoke of. He waited patiently for the Winemaker to continue; in a morbid way, hoping to understand why. Seconds ticked by, and Joe sat patiently. Finally, the Winemaker started slowly. He spoke so quietly Joe struggled to hear the words that were spoken from only a few feet away. "Sorry, I just have a hard time with certain things, such as death. I've had my run-ins with the Grim Reaper twice now, and have caused even more."

Time stopped while Joe tried to wrap his head around what the Winemaker had just said. What does he mean run-ins with the reaper, and caused even more? These words made no sense to Joe coming from a man who would catch a spider and release it outside, never hurting anyone or anything. The silence was deafening, and hundreds of questions and thoughts raced through Joe's mind. The Winemaker composed himself and said, "Let's go check on the grapes," and without a pause got up and walked out of the office, heading towards the fermenting grapes. Joe remained for a few moments, trying to understand what had just happened; the curiosity about the Winemaker's past was torturing him, and he didn't know why.

As if nothing at all had happened, they performed a quick punch down and then started to measure the fermentation process. The temperatures and specific gravity of each bin were measured and recorded in a log. Each bin was slightly different, but the general trend was good. Over the last few days, the sugar levels had dropped at a fairly good rate, and the temperature was okay, but not great. The Winemaker had a slightly concerned look on his face as he measured each bin. "What's the worry, Zen Master?"

"These bins are moving slower than I want, and the temperature is low. It is always a nervous time when we get down to about 7% sugar. As the yeast eats the sugar, the alcohol content rises, which is toxic to the yeast. Too much alcohol or not enough nutrients cause the yeast to shut down or die. If they do, we have what is called a 'stuck fermentation.' Typically, the yeast will happily eat the sugar until it is all gone, but sometimes things don't go smoothly. The temperature of the bins should be higher – this indicates that the yeast population is healthy and thriving. But our temperatures are on the cooler side, which indicates that the process is sluggish. If it gets too sluggish, the yeast can emit a Prion, which is a protein that tells the other yeast to also shut down. Bet you didn't know that a single-celled organism could communicate with billions of its friends? We are going to have to watch these bins very carefully over the next few days and hope the yeast don't die." With the mention of death again, the Winemaker's mood seemed to drop slightly.

Joe was going crazy and wanted to ask directly what was going on. But he felt it would be better to take the indirect route and ask a more subtle series of questions.

"So, how did you get your name?" Joe asked with an upbeat pitch.

In a deadpan tone, the Winemaker said, "My mother named me...."

This confused Joe, who had been expecting a response about the winery. Seeing the smirk on the Winemaker's face, he understood, and they both laughed.

"Sorry, but you wouldn't believe how many people ask the same question the same way, and I always give the same response and get the same reaction. Sorry for taking a little pleasure in your discomfort."

Joe thought, Good: at least he is smiling. Maybe we can get some answers.

"Okay then Zen Master, how did you come up with the winery name, Koi Zen Cellars?"

"Now that is the proper question. Remember: ask silly questions and get silly answers. But this is a good story that I hope you enjoy. It all started about fifteen years ago. I had built a small koi pond in my back yard. The whole pond was one of those pre-fab ones about five-foot-long and maybe a foot and a half deep. We had four small koi and enjoyed the sound of the running water and watching the fish swim around. Every night when I got home from work, I would go out and feed those always hungry little mouths.

"One day I returned home in a really bad frame of mind. The stress of running a division of a tech company was building up and I was close to a breaking point. I could feel that something was about to snap. I wasn't living a very healthy lifestyle and had too many vices. Anyway, as I walked outside to feed the fish, I found a raccoon sitting in the pond as if it were a sushi bar/sauna. Two little hands holding the carcass of a half-eaten fish. Other fish remains were by his side.

"In an instant, my fury raged and I wanted to physically strangle that raccoon with my bare hands. Without thinking, I charged at the raccoon, screaming with my hand extended ready to grab this monster. The raccoon turned towards me, half of a fish still in its mouth, and stood up. The fish dropped. The raccoon hissed in the most menacing tone, causing me to pause and reconsider.

"I turned and ran away, looking for a more appropriate tool to dispatch the varmint. I grabbed a shovel from the garage, and when I returned the raccoon was gone. I was furious and frustrated and decided that this was the breaking point. Two fish were still alive. One was scratched up but okay.

"I put down the shovel and called my second in command and told him I was taking two weeks off starting tomorrow. Being the boss has its advantages," he smirked. "The next day I grabbed the shovel and started to dig a deeper and bigger pond. I dug and dug in the San Diego soil, which is a mixture of clay and rock. Often, I had to use a digging bar to loosen a mere cup of dirt. But for a week I dug and dug and dug. My hands were blistered and my skin was tanned. My muscles were sore but there was something very cathartic about all of that digging. The next week pipes were laid, the concrete block walls were built and the rubber liner was laid out. Digging a simple hole helped to heal the blackness inside of me.

"Years went by, and the pond was now large enough and deep enough to keep out any creature. The fish had grown and spawned, and the pond became a place of refuge. After a long day at the office, Lisa and I would sit by the pond listening to the running water and watching the fish lazily swim around –

always interested in food. We would enjoy our glasses of wine and try to relax.

"In the morning I would sit by the side of the pond feeding the fish and drinking my cup of coffee. I often told my employees that I would 'talk to my fish each morning,' but it was my form of meditation. When I left tech, and Lisa and I decided to open the winery, we decided to create a place that was warm, inviting and calming. We wanted to create a place where people could come and relax and get away from the stress of the day. One day, Lisa said, 'It should feel like sitting around the pond.' And that became the theme of the winery.

"When I tell this story to people I often say, 'We thought about names like Fish Poop or Pond Scum, but we ended up with Koi Zen Cellars.' The 'Koi' part represents courage, perseverance, strength of purpose and good luck. The 'Zen' part is about gaining wisdom through direct experience and becoming the best you can be by choosing the middle path and helping others.

"Our motto is 'Helping others one glass at a time,' and every day we try to take a step closer to that goal. It is our lighthouse, the constant beacon that gives us direction even in stormy seas."

As much as Joe enjoyed the story, to his dismay it didn't answer any of the questions that he had in his mind, so he decided to take one more poke at it. "You said you were in tech. What did you do?" he asked innocently.

The air immediately turned cold. The Winemaker said, "I don't want to talk about it now," and walked away, leaving Joe feeling guilty but not knowing why.

Joe just couldn't leave things be, and he spent the rest of the night cyberstalking the Winemaker, to no effect. With little to no social media footprint, the backstory of the Winemaker would remain a mystery, at least for the night.

Darius Miller

CHAPTER 16

Weeks had gone by and Joe was no closer to figuring out what he wanted to do with his life than the day he first walked into the winery. The life lessons he had learned had changed his thinking, but the future remained a great mystery to him. The tension in the office was building and everyone was on edge. Something big was about to happen and Joe had a feeling that he was going to be directly impacted by these changes, but in one respect, he didn't care. He knew that his time had come to leave. He wasn't in any hurry, but inside he felt sure of himself – that is, until he started to think about not having a job, paycheck, or a place to go to every day.

He had wrapped up his work as usual by 1:00 and decided that it was a good time to 'get some fresh air.' He packed up his lunch box and briefcase and snuck out the door. First stop, the winery, of course, to check in on the progress of the fermentations and to catch up on what was coming up.

As he approached the winery, he saw a large tour bus parked out front and a tour group of twelve or so wandering into the winery. Joe quietly followed them in and took up a seat away from the crowd, but close enough to listen in. Becky was behind the bar ready to lead this journey on their zen steps of wine tasting. She was an expert at giving a fantastic presentation, and the group was going to eat it up.

With his back turned towards the crowd, Joe hung on every word that Becky was saying. She began, "The first step is to 'see' your wine." And as she explained the whole process, Joe began to drift away, thinking back over how far he had come over the last few weeks. He saw things differently now. He understood that there were always different sides to every situation. He saw how his actions and inactions directly caused 'ripples,' as Suzie had explained to him. He saw the stress at the office and the nervous behaviors of his co-workers. He saw where he had come and reflected on the choices he had made in the past, and how they caused him to be exactly where he was today. He could see that there was little chance of a future once his office merged with the other company. And he could see that, without a lighthouse to follow, he was adrift in the currents of life.

Becky continued, "The next zen step is to 'swirl.'" Joe reflected on how the new experiences of the last few weeks had opened his eyes. He no longer felt trapped in his head, and he was now more open and willing to take on new encounters and challenges than he had ever been before. By mixing things up, he was no longer a zombie pushing the same stack of paper every day. He understood that the world was large and that it was more full of abundance than he had ever thought. He felt the rush of excitement and curiosity in exploring new things, going to new places and thinking new thoughts. He had mixed up his work routine and now was highly efficient, allowing him the time and space to explore new thoughts and ideas. He was able to spend more time on self-care and learning than he ever had before; he was happy, Mary was happy and Lucy was always happy – the joy of being a child.

The tour group was highly engaged with Becky as she started the next segment. "The third zen step of wine tasting is to 'smell.'" Joe reflected on how three weeks ago, he never smelled anything, and now he was smelling everything: he smelled spices, flowers, dirt, rock – everything. The more he smelled, the better his sniffer got. Weeks ago, he thought he had a bad sniffer, but now he felt he had a much better nose. By remembering what he smelled, a whole new sensory world opened for him. The more he smelled, the more he could identify what he was smelling, which amazed Mary and Lucy.

He could smell a dirty diaper instantly from across the room – which unfortunately caused him to change a whole lot more diapers than before – but he was still happier with this newfound sensory organ he had forgotten years ago.

He also began to use the metaphor of 'when something doesn't smell right' more than ever before. Just as his nose could detect spoiled food, he senses could detect something wrong in the environment. The thing that constantly didn't smell right was the merger: that whole thing just was bad, and Joe wondered if he was the only one who thought so. Joe tensed in anticipation for the next zen step, which he had never heard presented before.

After everyone had completed their lesson on the proper zen way to smell their wine, Becky filled their empty glasses with the next wine sample and started on the fourth zen step – sipping.

"So, it may sound silly, but today we are going to learn how to sip the proper way, the zen way. At Koi Zen Cellars we are all about being mindful and in the moment. So, we are going to slow down a little and tune our focus in on tasting. So many people come into the winery thinking about the past or worrying about the future and aren't present in the moment. Sometimes they are busy chatting with their friends and just slam the wine down, not even thinking about what they are doing. But not today. Today we are going to be in the moment and are going to be mindful. But, before we begin, we must learn a whole new set of terms to describe what wine tastes like."

Becky reached behind the bar and pulled out two small paper plates and two salt shakers. She shook out a small pile from the first shaker that looked like salt onto the plate and began her explanation. "Wine is a remarkable substance. There are very few food products that can remain shelf-stable without pasteurization, refrigeration or major preservatives for decades like wine can. One of the reasons that wine can age so well is due to the acid content. Wine is a very acidic solution, and spoilage microbes don't like acidic solutions. One of the primary types of acid in wine is tartaric acid, and on the plate is a sample of tartaric acid. So, everyone, press your fingertip into the pile of acid and taste it." A young lady in a sundress was closest to the plate, and she looked at Becky with trepidation. "Don't worry, it won't hurt you, or taste bad. Just give it a try."

The young lady timidly dabbed her finger into the small pile and then tasted it. She scrunched her nose slightly but signaled that everything was okay. "Now, don't think too much about the tastes, but think about the sensation that happens in your mouth." The plate was passed from person to person, each timidly tasting and trying tartaric acid.

"So, what does acid do on the palate?" Becky asked. An older lady a few places down said it most succinctly, "It causes your mouth to salivate."

"That's right. The acid in wine causes you to salivate, and makes the wine feel bright and refreshing. If a wine has too much acid, it will cause you to drool, and without enough acid, it will taste flat, flabby or boring." Everyone shook their heads in acknowledgment.

"The next primary reason that wine can sit on a shelf for decades is due to the tannins. Tannins come from the skins, seeds, and stems of the grapes, and have a contrasting effect on your palate." Becky sprinkled a light brown powder onto the second paper plate and passed to the young lady in the sundress. She dabbed her finger and tasted it, scrunching up her face in a puckered look. Becky continued, "As you might have guessed, tannins dry your mouth out. An overly tannic wine makes you feel parched and looking for a glass of water.

Since red wines are fermented with the skins and seeds, they often have higher tannin content than white wines, which are not fermented with those things. Tannins are a natural anti-microbial, anti-bacterial and anti-oxidant, and likewise help keep the spoilage microbes away.

"The third line of microbial defense wine has is the alcohol content. Microbes don't like alcohol. Too little alcohol in a bottle of wine will cause it to taste thin and too much alcohol will make the wine taste hot, like a shot of vodka. The right amount of alcohol will give the wine body and structure. The more alcohol, the more body the wine will have, and alcohol is often perceived as sweet."

The group, including Joe, were enjoying the presentation and kept reaching for their wine sample, but Becky held them off. "Okay guys, just a few more terms and then you can dive in – mindfully, that is. The next quality of a wine is sweetness – referring to how much sugar is in the wine. Wines can range from bone-dry, zero sugar, to very sweet dessert and ice wines, that may have up to 20% sugar content. The standard terms used to describe sweetness would be dry, off-dry, semi-sweet and sweet. Most table wines fall into the dry and off-dry camp. Craft wines such as what Koi Zen Cellars produce tend to be on the bone-dry to dry side, while most commercial off-the-shelf wines tend to have a fair amount of residual sugar. Wines with sugar are easier to drink, but dry wines pair better with food.

"The next term is the fruitiness. When a wine has a lot of fruit notes, sometimes the palate will perceive the wine to be sweet, when it is completely dry. If you are unsure of whether a wine is fruity or sweet, there is a simple test you can do – hold your nose. If you hold your nose and you taste sweetness, then there is sugar. If the sweetness goes away, then it is just fruity.

"Using the descriptors of acidity, tannins, body, and fruit, it is easy to find the perfect wine for your taste. For example, think of a wine that is off-dry, medium body, light tannin, and high acidity versus a dry, full-body, high tannins and medium acidity. I am sure you can all 'taste' the difference between these wines in your mind. Once you get this concept down, pairing and ordering wines become a breeze, but that is another day and another class. You all have waited long enough, now I will explain how to sip wine!

"When you are evaluating a wine, it is good to become very focused on what you are doing. You can learn so much about a glass of wine – and life – if you are constantly present and critical of your senses. So, the zen way to 'sip' is to take about a half a tablespoon of wine into your mouth and swirl it around for a few seconds. The first reaction to the wine will be the temperature, then the acids and tannins will kick in, and then the fruit. Since almost everything you are tasting is a smell, some people will purse their lips and draw air into their mouths causing a little chirping sound while they are swishing the wine around. This requires a little coordination not to drip or drool, but allows air to enter the mouth, causing the wine aromas to move up into the back of the throat and into the nasal cavity."

Having been given a full lesson, set of instructions and building anticipation, everyone finally took their first zen sip of wine. Some drooled, some dripped, some were shocked and some were enlightened. Joe just sat there wishing he had a glass of wine to share the experience with. Have to plan a little bit better, Joe, he mused.

While the group was comparing notes, Joe began to realize the relevance of the proper way to taste wine – it wasn't just wine, it was a lesson in life. The simple act of a sip was more complicated and intricate if done mindfully and not absentmindedly. The myriad detail of each small sip, experience, thought, or feeling was astronomical. No amount of words could ever fully describe the simplest action or event. The depth and breadth were truly amazing, and unfortunately, so many people pass these experiences, and often their entire lives, unaware of 'reality.' At that moment Joe realized the sheer depth and mystery of life when one lives in reality and not illusion. No amount of words could ever completely describe even the most trivial experience, and one can only truly know through direct experience, and not from another description.

At that moment, Joe realized that he was on a new path, a path that still did not have a destination (other than the final destination we must all face). He was eager, he was excited and he was motivated to begin to truly begin to experience life to the fullest. How he was going to do this remained unclear.

Joe was still in deep thought when the Winemaker gently put his hand on his shoulder, causing him to jump. "So sorry, I didn't mean to startle you."

"That's okay. I was just thinking about what Becky was talking about – the zen way of sipping wine – and how it all relates to life. Do you have a few minutes? I could use a sounding board. There is so much on my mind and I just can't seem to make any progress."

The Winemaker nodded. He led Joe into the production area, pulled up two chairs and sat down, gesturing for Joe to do the same. "What's on your mind?"

Joe stumbled, made a false start, and then started again. The Winemaker just sat, quiet and attentive, allowing Joe to express himself the best he could. After laying out the basics of the company merger, his position and department being threatened, and his desire to do something different, he finally asked, "Why the winery? Why did you open Koi Zen Cellars?"

The Winemaker took a moment and composed his thoughts. Then he began.

CHAPTER 17

"It was almost thirty-five years ago when Lisa and I attended our first wine festival. She was an independent consultant for the Pennsylvania Beef Council and we were serving beef rouladen by the pound to a hungry crowd at the first annual Pennsylvania Wine Festival. I came to support her. We had been making beef rouladen for three days, but it was a bright spring day in the Pocono Mountains, so we took a break and went on our first-ever wine tasting.

"We strolled until we found a vendor who didn't have a line, and we approached. Lisa said, 'Can I try your White Zinfandel?'"

"The young man politely responded, 'Ma'am, that's a California grape.' This statement completely confused us, and he continued, 'Different grapes grow in different regions. This is all Pennsylvania wines, and unfortunately, we do not grow Zinfandel. But we have a wide range of wines from sweet to dry that you are welcome to try.'

"For the next twenty minutes, he poured wine after wine, explaining the nuances and helping us determine what we liked. His name was Tony, and he became a good friend. We shared many glasses of wine and parties together. He eventually moved to the west coast to follow a dream and became the executive chef for some major Hollywood actors. Anyway, we fell in love with the wine tasting experience and our passion for wine began to grow.

"Living on the east coast offered limited tasting opportunities, but when we moved to California years ago, our wine education exploded. There were so many wineries and places to visit. The more we tasted the more we learned, and the deeper our connection with wine was forged. Lisa and I

131

would put pictures of vineyards and wineries on our vision boards, and one day this dream manifested itself."

The Winemaker became very quiet for a moment - as if struggling with a decision. Eventually, he said, "I don't tell many people this – it's pretty personal information – but for some reason, I feel it's important to share with you now. It was 2012, a big year. My twin daughters turned eighteen and graduated from high school. Lisa and I celebrated twenty-five years of marriage and we both turned fifty. We spent three weeks in Europe having the best time. Life was good and we were living large, until two weeks after returning, when my world exploded: I was 'right-sized' out of a position along with my entire department. I was devastated. Within moments, I had lost my title, my status, my paycheck, and my identity. In an instant, I was a nobody, rejected and thrown out like the trash. Fifteen years of busting my ass, for what? Nothing.

"I slipped into a deep depression. I knew that going back to corporate would kill me, and a year and a half later it almost did. I was lost, burned out, confused and angry with everything. My kids were off at college and my life was quickly spiraling into the toilet.

"Then one Sunday morning I woke up feeling a bit off. You know when you wake up and your arm or leg is asleep? Well, it was like that, but it was my entire right side. I just slept funny; it will go away, I thought, but it never did. All day long I didn't say a word, hoping for the best, but the best never came.

"Unknown to Lisa, I went to the doctor's office the next day, where I was promptly taken into an examination room after describing my symptoms. A young tech came in and tried to take my blood pressure. She expertly placed the cuff on and pumped and pumped and pumped. I thought my arm would pop off. Then she tried again, and then on the other arm. You could see the fear in her eyes, and then she said, 'I'm going to get the doctor' and quickly left the room. Moments later the doctor appeared and took my blood pressure again – twice. He made a casual comment on how my blood pressure was high, and there was a grave concern on his face. I explained that I got nervous around doctors, but he just shook his head, knowing it was serious. I asked what my blood pressure was; he said it was 220/190. I didn't know what that meant, but it sunk in when I glanced at the machine: the highest number on the dial was 230. I was about to pop.

"Almost casually, he said, 'I have a friend in the ER department across the street, I think you should go see him. Now.' I stood in the parking lot trembling, now fearing for the worst and taking long drags on what was to be my last cigarette ever. A young Indian doctor in the ER stood over me for the second time in my life saying, 'You're lucky, you should be dead.' Five days later I was released from the hospital with many jars of pills and a new outlook on life. The official diagnosis was a major stroke at the age of fifty-two.

"As I mentioned, that was my second encounter with the Grim Reaper. Let's just call it another wake-up call. Nicotine is one of the hardest substances to quit – scientists say it's more addictive than cocaine and heroin. But I was able to quit on the spot without ever going back. It is amazing what you can accomplish when you want something. In my case, my life was more important than my bad habits and the dead-end path I was on. Remember that Joe: everyone can be remarkable in what they do if they want it.

"I convalesced for the next few months and then Lisa and I decided to follow a dream we had for many years: to open a winery. And so we did, and here we are. You see Joe, no one knows when they are going to take their last breath, and so people often wait for the future to fulfill their desires, passions, and accomplishments – frequently never getting to realize them. This is a shame and one of the biggest wastes of life. What is your dream, Joe? What impact are you going to have on the universe during the few moments we all have in this small flash of existence?"

Not knowing any suitable answer, Joe tried to skirt the question by asking, "But how did you know you wanted to open the winery? Why not something else, and how did you know it would work?"

"Grasshopper, only the Master can answer a question with a question, but considering you did answer the question, I will forgive you. It is obvious that you are still lost in the fog and are seeking answers, so I will continue with my humble story and maybe it will inspire you to find your own lighthouse.

"Lisa and I had been interested in wine for over twenty-five years, but we were mere amateurs, not even enthusiasts and definitely not connoisseurs. We enjoyed fine wines but drank cheap wines most of the time. But we did have a dream of owning a winery. Pictures of wineries and vineyards dotted our vision boards, and it was something we both agreed on.

"However, the fantasy of owning a winery is very different from reality. In the fantasy, Lisa and I would be sitting on the veranda as the sun began to set across the vineyards, each vine pristine as field workers tended them. We sipped our chilled Chardonnay and relaxed. But that was a fantasy, and this, my friend, is a reality," he said, indicating the winery with an expansive sweep of his arm.

"But even though the reality is different than the fantasy, it is still our passion to serve people, and the winery gives me a chance to restore my karma in a more positive way. And to answer your final question, you will learn that when you are passionate and driven, you can accomplish anything that is realistic and that makes the world a better place. When you are driven with a fixed, firm purpose that is filled with compassion, it is hard to fail. Even in rough times, the universe will align and provide you with the support that you need – it is just one of those mysteries in life.

"But if your path is driven by selfishness, greed, arrogance, or other self-aggrandizing motivations like these, the universe will thwart you and try to twist you up and derail your intentions at every step. This is the fundamental belief the Buddha taught. And this is the root problem so many people have today in our modern society. They are on the wrong path – looking to acquire the wrong things for the wrong purpose. As I told my kids when they were young, 'Make wise choices.'"

Joe left the winery that night feeling inspired, but no closer to answering his calling. That would change soon enough.

Darius Miller

CHAPTER 18

Joe was running a little late the next day, and by the time he got to the office, it was buzzing with activity. As he wound his way through the cube maze, he passed Sally's empty office – she had quit two weeks ago to pursue her doctorate. Frank's cube was also empty: he had left a few days ago to work with his brother-in-law in the construction business, helping and learning about building codes and code compliance in preparation for returning to school to pursue his architecture degree in the spring. Teddy-bear George was also gone, now working at a yoga studio as an assistant and trying to find an accreditation program to complete – his dream was to go to Costa Rica for this.

Bob had left, and so had Alice. Half of the office had moved on, but Joe still wandered the labyrinth of half-empty cubes every day. Larry was busy at his desk pushing papers and trying to accomplish something, but it was like rearranging the deck chairs on the Titanic. He would go down with the ship and probably still not know why.

Joe finally arrived at his cube only to find Clark sitting in his guest chair waiting for him. "Running a little late today Joe?" he said with a smile.

Joe plopped down on his ergonomic swivel chair and spun around to face Clark. "What's up?"

"Hey, you can see what's going on around here, and it isn't looking good for us buddy. I hope you, of all people, realize this. People are leaving left and right, and management doesn't seem to care. No matter what I ask, I get no response from Loser Larry. I'm getting nervous about the future and what to do right now. I have so many crazy thoughts running through my head and I just need to talk to someone."

Joe leaned forward with interest, thinking about everything he had recently learned. He was excited to share the small amount of wisdom he had learned, and how to see the world differently. "Go ahead."

"Can you introduce me to the Winemaker?"

Joe sat back dejected, but within a few moments he had composed both himself and after a few texts, the plan was set, "Let's book out of the office at noon and go over to the winery. Larry is so out of touch with reality, he won't even notice."

"Thanks, man, this means a lot to me."

###

They arrived just before 1:00. It was still an hour before the winery opened, but the Winemaker had said he was going to be there. The other businesses were still open, so they had a hard time finding a parking spot, eventually getting one a few buildings away. During the brief walk, Joe gave a very brief background of how he was involved in the winery and what to expect. "Remember, the Winemaker can be very direct and think about your answers before answering. He always says, 'Ask stupid questions and get stupid answers.'"

The front door was unlocked, and like everyone else, Clark was amazed at the interior. Most of the lights were still off, casting the place in an intriguing gloom. It was the end of the harvest season and most of the fruit was pressed off, but one batch of Zinfandel was still in a tank waiting for pressing. The aromas of fermentation weren't as strong as before, but there was no doubt that this was a fully functioning winery making wine right in the middle of the community. Joe showed Clark around, and they poked here and there looking for the Winemaker. They found him tucked deeply within a stack of barrels, precariously perched ten feet in the air as he replaced a bung that had popped off. He tossed the dirty bung to Joe, and Joe instinctively sanitized it and tossed it back.

"Every day we have to check all of the bungs," he said, holding the rubber cork Joe had just tossed up to him. "Sometimes the wine is still fermenting, which causes pressure to build up in the barrels, or MLF is still happening, which also causes CO_2 to build up and shoot these suckers across the room. A friend of mine had a bung shoot right through the roof – well, skylight. I'll be down in a moment, so go grab a glass of wine and relax."

Clark scanned the tasting sheet and selected the Syrah from Santa Barbara.

"Good choice Clark – although it's impossible to pick a bad wine here; they're all excellent." Joe snuck behind the bar, ignoring the "Employee's Only" sign, and fetched two glasses, pouring himself a Cabernet Sauvignon and the Syrah for Clark, just as the Winemaker rounded the corner. He just smiled and proceeded to the kitchen, returning a few moments later with a beer.

"A beer?" Clark said in surprise. "Why not a glass of wine? Aren't you a winemaker?"

Joe intervened, "If you sampled wine all day, wouldn't you want something else?" The Winemaker just smiled and settled into a comfortable red swivel chair placing his beer on the table. The other two joined him, Joe on the couch and Clark on a padded straight-backed chair. Everyone enjoyed their beverage in silence for a few moments, and then the Winemaker asked, "So Clark, Joe said you wanted to meet me. What do you want to talk about?"

Clark sat there for a painfully long time, fidgeting with his hands and glass, making false starts and being unable to get any words out. Tears welled in the corner of his eyes, and he avoided eye contact. The tension in the room was unbearable, and it felt like something was going to burst. The Winemaker just stared at Clark with an intense look as if he was seeing the thoughts directly inside of Clark's head. Joe had flashbacks of the old Vulcan mind meld that Spock would do in the old Star Trek series of the late 1960s.

The tension became uncomfortable for Joe, who was both intrigued and a touch scared of what the next words would be.

The Winemaker broke the silence with a joke. "Two monks were walking back to the monastery after attending a silent retreat, when they happened to meet a beautiful woman standing at the bank of a river. She was obviously in distress, and explained that she needed to cross the river, but couldn't get her dress wet. Without thinking any further of it, the elder monk swooped her up and carried her across the stream, and the monks continued their path home. After a few miles, the younger monk turned to the elder and said, 'How could you have touched that woman? We are bound by our vows of chastity.' There was a long pause, and then the elder replied, 'I put her down on the opposite bank long ago, but you are still carrying her after all of these miles.'"

Clark and Joe both looked at the Winemaker, confused by the old parable. "Clark, you are carrying a heavy burden that should have been put down a long time ago. What is done is done, and no matter how many times you think about it, it will not change."

The air was thick with emotional strain and tears welled in Clark's eyes. Almost inaudibly, he began his saga. "I have never spoken about this, for almost thirty years now, but every night I awake in terror from what I am about to tell you.

"I once was a soldier. But not any ordinary soldier. I was Special Ops. I was also only a few months past my nineteenth birthday. While all my friends were home partying and getting laid, I was in a foreign country doing the unthinkable. For months they had trained us, honed us and beat the crap out of us so that, no matter what happened, we would be able to deal with it. We were lean and mean and ready for action.

"One day we were told to go check out this house where it was suspected that they were making bombs. We were young and eager and willing to do anything for our country. We approached the house in the middle of BFE. It was no more than a dirt shack: the roof was about to collapse, there was no plumbing and piles of crap littered the road. The walls were made from dirt and scraps of wood, and there were dozens of chickens all running around pecking at this and that. A bit of corrugated steel roof panel was the front door. The whole team was hustled outside this place, ready to pounce.

"Tensions were high and everyone was nervous but silent – completely silent. All you could hear were those damn chickens clucking here and there, or a dog barking in the distance. Everyone was armed to the gills and we were prepared. Maybe over-prepared: pumped full of adrenaline, locked and loaded, waiting for the final signal to breach the door. Time stopped when the first lieutenant gave the signal to breach the building. In perfect formation, we poured through that piece of sheet metal, checking left and right, calling out clear signals.

"There was a total of six rooms in this small abode, but the building was clear. There was no one there and no bomb-making supplies could be found. The tension was still high, but the team started to exit the building. I was the last to exit. Just as I reached the door, there was the faintest noise and a movement to the side. After months of training, reflexively my combat knife was in my hand and I struck. I felt the knife make contact, and heard this horrible gurgling sound only to see her..." Clark completely lost his composure. He was weeping while thumping his fists into his thigh as if hurting himself could fix the past.

"Clark, stop: we all understand what happened. No need to explain more."

Joe sat there stunned, not knowing what to say, think or feel. The worst thing that had ever happened to him was a fender bender and a parking ticket.

After a few minutes, the Winemaker, said, "Clark, what is done is done. It is time to move on. Bad things happen to good people and good people do bad things. That is just who we are, and all we can try to do is to make the world just a little bit better. You have beat yourself up enough over something you had little control of. You were trained, you were equipped, you were placed in a bad situation, and you did exactly what you were told to do. How can you berate yourself for following someone else's orders?"

"But I stabbed…"

"Enough! Enough of the past and the excuses of not moving forward. The only question I have is, what are you going to do moving forward? If you can't answer that question, then there is no hope."

The Winemaker stood up, tears in his eyes, and walked away into the depth of the stack of barrels. Something had touched a nerve in the Winemaker.

Joe and Clark sat in silence for another twenty minutes. When the staff started arriving, Clark looked up to Joe and said, "I'm lost."

Joe replied, "So am I."

Joe and Clark spent a lot of time together over the next week at the office. Their regular lunch crew had all moved on, and they now spent their break talking about feelings, fears, and possibilities. Clark was making some progress, but Joe still felt that he was missing something obvious that needed to be accomplished before he moved on to the next chapter of his life.

Clark spilled his innermost thoughts and talked about his demons while they sat in the lunchroom or the park across the street. Clark turned out to be a very passionate and thoughtful person, who was hiding behind a shell of indifference and non-commitment. Neither of them could figure out a path forward, but they were there to support each other during the shifting times.

Each day the office became more and more of a ghost town, as people bailed left-and-right, leaving management scrambling to keep revenue up and customers happy with a skeleton staff. From the top to the bottom, and from each side of the two merging companies, it was clear that this 'synergy' was destructive, with both companies losing key personnel.

Thirteen days after Clark met the Winemaker, he announced to Joe that he was moving on. His incident of years gone by had left a deep scar that needed to be healed. He and Joe were sitting by the side of the pond when he asked, "Joe, can you explain karma to me?"

Joe sat there for a few moments collecting his thoughts and trying to figure out the best way to communicate a complicated concept to someone who was so deeply troubled by the past. He took his time and spoke very slowly, using very clear language and a soft supportive tone. "Many people think that karma is a good-versus-bad rating system: if you do good then good things happen, and if you do bad things, then bad things happen. But I have come to believe that's not right at all."

Joe picked up a rock and skipped it across the still pond, watching the ripples form and expand. "Every action changes the universe; this was explained to me by a great woman – Suzie from Crush Crew. We all are on a path or a course of action. Now suppose that you were a drug dealer living in the slums. There is a lot of violence surrounding you, and the chances that you will be involved in some incidents are very high. It is not directly because of the actions that you will be punished, but the situation that you live in. Now imagine, on the other hand, that you are a relief worker helping people in a disaster. In that situation, no matter how badly you mess up, it would probably still be better for the situation.

"In the first case, you are almost guaranteed to get involved in something unwholesome, where in the second case it is hard not to be a benefit.

"This is how I think of karma. Many people blame the situation they are in on external factors. They are scared to admit that they made poor choices or that they are free to move on. They fail to take responsibility for the situation – not what they have done, but the situation. They fail to realize that they have the power to change if they want to.

"That's the hard part. Knowing what should be done and doing it. As they say, 'Talk is cheap,' but doing is putting yourself out there where you might make a mistake, or even cause harm. But if your intentions are wholesome and clear, then you will turn out okay.

"In your case, you were put into a horrible situation and you did the best job you could at the time. Karma isn't against you, and there are no black stripes on your record. You did what you were trained and told to do. You followed orders and things went bad. But things often go bad. Think about all the tornadoes, or hurricanes, fires, earthquakes and such. Bad things happen no matter how 'good' we act. That's just part of life.

"The trick here is to figure out two things: what are your options, and how are you going to make it better? I think this is the heart of the question the Winemaker asked you a few days ago."

Clark picked up a small pebble and tossed it into the pond. He watched the ripples expand around the small splash and said, "I could help."

"Help what?"

"People, I could help people. For years I have been living in this shell. At first, it was to protect me from the outside, but then it became a shell to protect the outside from me. By closing down, I didn't have to think about much of anything. I worked, got paid, paid my bills and then did it repeatedly. Days came and days went and if I stayed numb, then nothing bothered me.

"But now that doesn't seem like the right path to be on. I did some bad things in the past and that is something I will probably never get over, but it doesn't have to be a roadblock keeping me from moving on. And as you explained, or what I understood about how you feel about karma, then helping others would be a good step forward, wouldn't you agree?"

They spent a lot of time together over the next week, each sharing personal thoughts and feelings, trying to work through the past while trying to move into the future. The more Joe got to understand Clark, the more he realized that down deep he was a compassionate and loving guy who derailed his life all because of a very traumatic bad experience. He began to realize that Clark was moving through life as a ghost, dead inside and afraid to be alive. Joe continually encouraged him to move on, and bit by bit they were making collective progress, each dealing with their own personal demons that lurked in the corners of their minds.

A few days later, Clark disappeared without a word. He never returned to the winery, nor ever talked to the Winemaker again. Six months later, the Winemaker and Joe both received a simple postcard with a picture of an elephant and a humble village. Clark was using his military training to be a first responder as part of the Peace Corps, being deployed into impacted areas, whether it was from fire, flood, famine, war or disease. The card read, "I'm healing by giving."

CHAPTER 19

Thanksgiving came and went. Joe's universe was in a tizzy before Christmas, and the merger still had not happened. There was problem after problem, but the merger kept going forward incredibly slowly. Each day a new cube became vacant and the office grew quieter and quieter. All of Joe's lunch crew and friends were gone. All moving on, taking that next step, making it big; but Joe was still there.

Day after day he arrived, a little late, with his lunchbox and a smile. He left each day with an empty lunchbox and a smile. Even after all this time, he was still no closer to his next step than he had been before he met the Winemaker. Everyone else had moved on, but not him, and he didn't know why. Koi Zen was busy with holiday events and parties, which left very little time or space to learn at the winery. Two weeks into December, Joe received a simple email.

Hey Crush Crew:

The final press has happened and now it is time for the wine, Winemaker and his loyal crew to sleep for the winter. But there is one more task to accomplish, and that is the Crush Crew Party!

Next Saturday at 4:00 pm, our house – bring a friend. Plenty for everyone

Cheers,

Winemaker

Joe read and re-read the email repeatedly. 'Average Joe' was invited to the Winemaker's house for a party. There was only one problem: Mary and Lucy were out of town visiting Mary's mom on the east coast, and he had no date!

Joe was in a panic. The Winemaker used very few words, and he said explicitly "bring a friend." If the Winemaker said it, it must be important. Joe was in a pinch, with only a few days to find a friend. All his friends had moved away, onto new paths, filled with new opportunities and new experiences. Suddenly Joe had nobody.

The next morning, Joe was walking to his cube when Larry called out, "Joe, wait a minute. We need to talk."

All the blood in Joe's body froze that instant. He knew that he had been busted. His mind flashed through all of those sick days, all the long lunches and all the days he left early. As casually as he could, he popped his head into Larry's office and said, "What's up?" His heart was racing and he could feel his blood pressure rising as his hands began to shake.

"Joe, I have to make a call in about three minutes, but we really do need to talk. It's very important and is going to impact both of us. Can you stop back in about an hour?"

Joe could barely squeak the words out, "Sure, Larry, no problem."

He meandered his way to his cube and sat down heavily. He knew the end was in sight, and even though the ship was sinking, he just couldn't bale – not yet. Why? He didn't know. He began to meditate right there in his cube. He closed his eyes and slowed down his breathing, slowly counting from one to ten and incrementing with every inhalation. His belly moved out with an in-breath and in when he exhaled. He could feel his beating heart slow and the muscles in his back and neck begin to relax.

He needed to gain his composure and prepare himself to be accountable for all his transgressions; his meeting was in forty-five minutes. As he relaxed deeper into meditation, he began reflecting on the last few months and how he had changed, just not moved on. He thought about the first time he walked into Koi Zen Cellars, and how the outside was drab and uninspiring, but the inside was magical. It was magical the way it looked, and the people who frequented it. It was magical because of the bonding and reconnecting people did with their dates, or spouses, or friends.

It was magical how he was now beginning to see things differently. He no longer fantasized about the future or dwelt on the past. He tried very hard to be in the moment and to experience life in the here and now. His meditations helped him become focused and allowed him to understand his own biases, prejudices, and habits. This mind watching the mind made him act more responsibly, rather than reactively, and he knew that he was a better person now.

His mind's eye drifted around the nearly empty office space, thinking about his friends that had moved on. He was truly happy for them, knowing that in the past he would have been jealous, thinking that he could never catch a break and that life was always better someplace else. Now he was taking responsibility for his actions. Soon he would be facing Larry. He didn't know how the conversation would turn out, but even this he faced with equanimity.

He knew that he needed to move on, to use the lessons that he had learned at the winery over the last few weeks, but something was holding him back. Intellectually, he knew what his fate would be at the end of the hostile merger, but in his gut, he just couldn't move on – not yet, at least. Something was holding him back, as if there was still a task to finish, or mission to accomplish. What it was, he just didn't know, so he stayed day after day watching the ship sink.

He thought about Suzie, who had transformed her life by passing up the big paycheck and status to help save animals.

She had taught him about how to create good ripples in the universe rather than negative ripples. She taught him that passion was more important than money, but he was still trying to fully grasp that concept.

He thought about Sally, who would soon be a doctor helping to find a cure for cancer, to honor her father who passed away so many years ago. She had the courage to step up and take that bold new path. She was brave enough to face the unknown.

He thought about Frank, who moved on, trying to follow his dream to be an architect. When Frank talked about designing museums and cathedrals, Joe couldn't help but be caught up in the passion and the burning desire that Frank emanated. Joe wished he had just a little spark – something small, something to build on to move forward into the unknown.

He thought about big old teddy bear George who was on his way to be a yoga teacher. The thought of this giant mass teaching a class of lean, lithe young females made Joe smile. He just couldn't imagine what George would look like in the downward dog pose, but he was sure one day he would see a post on social media.

He thought about Clark and the many deep dark emotional conversations that they had shared, the secrets and fears that they both carried. He thought about how he'd felt when Clark disappeared without warning, fearing for the worst but hoping for the best (he was still working on being more stoic).

He thought about Bob and the last time he saw him when they accidentally bumped into each other at the winery. Bob was now teaching guitar lessons to underprivileged kids and singing lessons to abused women in the hopes that they could once again find happiness in life.

He thought about Mary and her desire to teach small children. She was enrolled in two classes at the local college earning her teaching credentials. It might take some time for her to complete the classes since she wanted to spend at least the first year home with their unborn son Jack.

All these people were part of Joe's life, and all had moved on except for him. But in about thirty minutes he would face Larry, and there was a good chance that he would be forced to move on, whether he wanted to or not. He thought deeply about his actions. He knew he wasn't an ideal employee, but he was a good employee. He had worked hard and done his time. He never complained about the tasks or workload. When he was behind, he stayed late without complaining, and he rarely ever made a mistake.

He was proud of his work, but felt completely uninspired. The last five years had in some ways been a complete waste of time. New policies came and old policies went. He was doing the same menial tasks on day one as day 1500. He thought about his eulogy: "Here lies Average Joe. He came and he went and no one noticed or cared."

He glanced at his clock. There were just a few moments before he had to meet with Larry. He went to the restroom and, on the way, his hands began to shake and his blood pressure soared. He was too nervous to pee and splashed some cold water on his face. The face in the mirror looked scared, but he pulled it together and was going to stand up for himself. In a flash he decided: he was going to tell Larry off and quit, right there on the spot, and give Larry a good tongue lashing just because! With shoulders drawn back and chest puffed out, he marched out of the restroom on a mission to face Larry.

As his hand touched the door jamb of Larry's office, all the steam when out of him and he became meek. "Knock, knock, it's Joe."

"Oh, Joe. Thanks for coming by. Please close the door and have a seat," he said with a forced smile and welcoming gesture.

Joe began to tremble, wondering where all the gusto and guts he had in the restroom had gone. With a shaky hand, he closed the door and fumbled to sit down in the chair directly across from Larry. "Larry, I know what this is about and I just want to say that..."

"Joe, stop. Please stop talking. I have to tell you something, and it isn't going to be easy, so please just hear me out, okay?"

Even though Joe hated his job and knew that he had to move on, he was scared and felt like he was going to lose it any second. Sheer terror raced through him for an instant. His heart beat faster and faster, his temples throbbed, his underarms began to sweat profusely, and his hands were stiff, cold and clammy. A giant lump formed in his throat, making it difficult to breathe. It was a full-blown panic attack, and he just wanted to die on the spot.

"Joe, I know that is will be difficult for you to understand, but you have been working for me for – what, two years now?"

"Five," Joe said quietly, his voice quivering. "It's been five years working for you."

"Okay, five years, but that doesn't matter. Even though we don't talk much, I respect the work you have done around here, and how you work with your teammates. But that isn't enough, I'm afraid. I also know that you don't care much for me. I know that you call me 'Loser Larry' behind my back, and..."

He paused for what seemed like an eternity. Called out this way, Joe wished the earth would open and swallow him up.

Larry continued, "And you're right!"

The words hung in the air like a giant purple elephant. Joe didn't know if he had heard Larry right or not, and he sat there in a state of shock. Larry sat back in his chair, looking meek and sad. Moments dragged on.

"I am a loser Joe, in more ways than you can imagine. I never wanted to be a department manager - or your boss! I don't know a damn thing about being a manager, but I got stuck with it and have hated it ever since. I don't know what I am doing half the time, and no one likes me. You think I am an asshole, and I am. Not because I want to be: I just don't deal with people well. I shouldn't be in this position.

"I'm the laughing stock of the whole division and have been for the last eight years. I hate my job probably even more than you do. All I hear from upper management is 'increase close rate,' 'increase retention,' 'decrease overhead,' 'work smarter not harder.' I don't know what that stuff means, so I just flounder around day after day trying to keep my head down and out of the picture as much as possible.

"Every day I run around scared that I'm going to get called out. But you know what? The higher-ups and the executives are even worse than me. Believe it or not, but it is true. Have you ever heard of the 'Peter Principle?'"

Joe, still in shock by this sudden turn of events and the confessions his boss was gushing, just shook his head no.

"It says that in most hierarchical organizations, people are promoted and rise to their level of incompetence. When people are good at something, they are promoted to higher positions, but they are often completely incompetent at completing the tasks in a higher position. Look at this whole merger: it is being orchestrated by a bunch of baboons. That's why it is so messed up. Well, I am Peter; a perfect example of Peter Principle."

Without taking a breath Larry launched again, "I don't even know how I became the manager of the 'Outbound Customer Fulfilment Operation.' What the hell is that? You guys sell insurance policies. I started with this company thirteen years ago in advanced software development. Do you know the Fit-Right program that you guys use – the one that optimally matches the policy to the customer? That's mine. I wrote it. It compares over 1200 data points per customer using heuristics, deep learning, and greedy optimization algorithms. My master's degree is in computer science, not management! I was writing deep learning algorithms even before they were a thing. I have also dabbled in neural networks, artificial intelligence, and latent semantic indexing analysis. I am no manager as much as you are a... hell, I don't even know what you are, Joe.

"I had been developing the Fit-Right program for five years. I was fresh out of grad school, full of advanced concepts and a tenacious work ethic. I would program for sixteen to twenty hours each day, seven days a week, and loved every second of it. Every bug, mistake, and false start was just one step towards the final solution. I wanted the Fit-Right program to be perfect. About seven years ago, we were close to deploying the Fit-Right program across the whole company, and they stuck me with training. I didn't know how to train people, but management figured that since I wrote it, I could explain it. Well, that was mistake number one. Just because you are good at it doesn't mean you can teach it or sell it. Anyway, I was working with Betty, the former boss of this department, training the staff. Things were going okay for about a year while we worked out the kinks and made system improvements based on feedback, but then she got sick. They found out she had ovarian cancer, and she left the company.

"Management, being so brilliant, said, 'Hey Larry, you are training the Outbound Customer Fulfilment Operation - you are the new department manager. Do a good job Larry and don't let us down,' and they walked away. Buffoons, complete and total buffoons.

"Joe, I'm in a pinch and I need your help."

Joe was still in shock, but this latest comment just went over the top. He needs my help?!

"Joe, you know I suck at being a manager, but that's the position I have been stuck in for the last seven years. I have lost track of tech, and feel I'm not qualified for that either. I'm thirty-seven years old and am still living in my mother's house. She passed away twenty years ago and left me burdened with a huge financial responsibility. She had been very sick, and she was the only thing that I had in my life other than programming, and my cats. If I lose my job, I'm going to be screwed. You might think that I'm an asshole and not want to help me, but I have seen you help others, the people in this office. I have seen you help them move on and become better people.

"Joe, can you help me? I'm begging you, please help me." Tears were rolling down Larry's cheeks, and he looked like a broken man. The façade of many years had finally broken, and he appeared humble. Joe's heart wrenched, and he didn't know what to say. He didn't think that he had helped his co-workers – he attributed that to the Winemaker – but then an idea flashed through his mind. "Hey Larry, what are you doing next Saturday? I have some friends I want you to meet."

CHAPTER 20

The evening air was crisp and the harsh yellow street lamps cast a garish light on the parking lot as Joe pulled into the winery. The place was hopping for a Wednesday. There was a private party at the upper bar for thirty people, and a mix of regulars and first visitors were learning about wine, tasting wine, sharing stores and reducing the midweek stress. Joe waved hello to Annie and Kasha. They were the nightly wine stewards, always eager with a smile, story, and pitch.

Joe wandered around looking for the Winemaker, finding him in the larger production area. The fermentation bins had all been taken off-site for storage, which left the floor wide open, except for the twenty-seven wine barrels the Winemaker had lined up on the floor.

Shrieks of a power washer could be heard in the distance, and the back ten-foot rollup door was ajar. Looking up, the Winemaker said, "Joe, great to see you. How's life?"

Now, a question like "How's life?" from the Winemaker had to be answered very carefully, and Joe took a moment to contemplate his thoughts. "Not bad, things are looking up," he said in a casual upbeat tone.

"Is that so?"

The question hung in the air. Things weren't good for Joe: his branch was closing, people were leaving, and he had no direction nor any form of a plan. All his work friends had moved on, but he was still there watching the ship sink, wondering if he would be sucked down in a great rush as the remains of the once large and thriving office quietly sank into oblivion.

The silence was deafening as Joe thought about his situation and how he was groping to answer the Winemaker's question.

Meanwhile, the Winemaker appeared oblivious to Joe's distress and was busy sampling each barrel of wine, taking notes and moving on to the next barrel. Avoiding the question, Joe asked, "What's going on?"

"Tonight, my friend, we are racking off this year's Syrah."

"What is 'racking off'?'"

"When you were here learning about pressing the wine off the must, do you remember how turbid the wine was?"

"Yeah, most of it was cloudy, except the wine at the end of the press cycle."

"The cloudiness comes from suspended solids and dead yeast cells. This 'mook' falls to the bottom of the barrels and starts to compact. Now, there are several ideas about this 'mook,' which is called 'gross lees.' Some winemakers will leave this in the barrel, some will stir the barrels to re-suspend the gross lees, and some will rack-off the lees, which we are doing right now.

"These dead yeast cells and suspended grape solids can enhance the texture and mouthfeel of the wine, and often give it a slightly nutty, bready or yeasty quality. However, sometimes if the gross lees have too many nutrients, bad microbes can start to give the wine a 'funk.' The most common 'funk' is a rotten egg smell produced by hydrogen sulfide. Even though it smells bad, by aerating the wine and racking-off, the smell will blow off and no one would ever know it even happened. But that isn't the only bad smell that can happen. There is another spoilage bacterium called Bret, which can smell like nail polish remover, barnyard, horse manure, wet rat, or musty. These spoilage smells are very difficult to remove if they can be removed at all.

"This Syrah was pressed about two weeks ago, and the gross-lees have fallen out and collected at the bottom. Now Syrah is a workhorse wine, and it's basically indestructible, but it does have a bad tendency to develop hydrogen sulfide – rotten egg – and an easy way to remove is it to rack-off."

"But what is racking-off?"

"What we do is very carefully siphon off the clear wine at the top, and leave the gunk at the bottom. Then we wash the barrel out with a power washer – that's what Dane is doing outside – and then fill the barrel again. Sometimes – well, vary rarely – a barrel doesn't taste as good as it should. When this happens, we don't want to mix that wine with the other wine, as this could cause the whole batch to be tainted. That is why it's important to taste the wine in each barrel and to smell each barrel after it has been thoroughly cleaned."

"Oh, I thought you were just drinking on the job," Joe joked.

The Winemaker responded, "I am, but each barrel is worth over $10,000, and one mistake could ruin the whole batch, so better to be safe than sorry."

Joe shut up, realizing that this was a serious business, but curiosity grabbed hold of him. "Can I taste with you oh great Master?" he asked, trying to create a little levity.

"Of course, Grasshopper…. Once you tell me your plan for the future."

Joe froze. He knew that he couldn't wiggle out of this conversation so easily.

"Go grab a glass and we can have a little chat about what's going in your life, Joe."

They were sampling barrel eight of twenty-seven and Joe was starting to relax. The Winemaker was spitting each sample out, while Joe was swallowing, trying to get his fortitude together to answer the Winemaker's simple question. The Winemaker just waited patiently for the right moment to express itself.

"I have been hanging out at the winery for a few months now and I have learned so much about wine, winemaking and myself. I used to be very wrapped up in my own head, always thinking and moving through life like a zombie or something.

"But you taught me how to 'see' the world through new eyes. I can recognize now when I zone out, not appreciating my surroundings. I can also see my thoughts and the biases that I have, and I now know the things I still need to work on.

"You taught me the value of 'swirling,' to let situations breathe, and to look at the situation from different perspectives, trying to understand more of what is really there, rather than just snapping to a judgment or falling into the same old habits, though I still have quite a few. I have learned that by looking at the same thing in different ways, new opportunities emerge and new things can be learned. I have lived with myself for thirty-two years, and now I am beginning to appreciate all the different facets of my life, such as being a husband, a father, a contributor, a friend, an employee, and a help to others in need.

"I have learned to 'sip' life by taking in each experience, digesting it and internalizing it. I am afraid that most of my life I lived in a fluff zone, not taking anything seriously. Yeah, I had my ups and downs, but I didn't really take it in – I just kind of brushed experiences off, the good ones and the bad ones, and moved on to the next shiny object in front of me. Now I want to dig deep and understand what is going on, to experience it and to be part of it. I want to internalize each experience and make it part of me.

"I am still meditating and taking better care of myself with fresh air, exercise and spending more time building my relationship with Mary and Lucy. I can accomplish more because I can focus on a task and see it through completion, instead of getting distracted. I am happier, Mary is happier and Lucy is just a joy to spend time with.

"At work, most of my friends have moved on, which is very sad, but I am not jealous. I am actually very happy for them. They are each following a new path. I just hope that the new path is what they want. I know that they will be my friends forever and I will be there for them if they ever stumble. This is something new: I have developed deep connections with them as I watched them transform, I just wish..."

"What do you wish Joe?"

There was a long awkward pause, "I wish I knew what my new path was. I am still looking for my lighthouse, the thing that will lead me forward, but I haven't found it yet. I am just drifting without purpose or direction."

"Grasshopper, you are missing the most important zen step. You must also learn how to 'savor' each experience. First you 'see' it, then you 'swirl' it, then you 'smell' it, then you 'sip' it and finally, you must 'savor' it. At this moment you combine the external with the internal and figure out how it matches. Did you like it, did you not like it? How did it make you feel? Would you do it again or not, and if so why? Without savoring, nothing is learned from the experience. This is something to think about Joe; in fact, it is the most important thing."

The air felt electric and heavy at the same time. Joe felt a thick buzz of energy that he couldn't explain.

Joe didn't make it to barrel twenty-seven but left the winery shortly after the Winemaker's statement. His mind was charged and random thoughts tore through his mind, no matter how much he tried to focus. A wave of thought, memories, emotions, and images raced through his mind like a crazy kaleidoscope of a drug-induced haze. He needed to think, reflect and assess this missing concept, for in it he hoped to find the key. A few moments later he was slowly walking around the pond at the park.

He walked in silent walking meditation focusing completely on the movement and feeling of each step: heel, toe, lift, swing, place, heel, toe repeatedly. Each step was slow, methodical and mindful. He could feel his pant leg brush his calf, the small crunch as his heel struck the stone path. He could feel the weight shifting from foot to foot. It took him ten minutes to reach the bench on the other side of the pond, though it was only 300 feet away.

His mind calmed, and when he reached the bench, he sat in half-lotus position under a fir tree. The pine needles were soft, but a few poked at him through his thin pants. The smell of resin, earth, and pond filled his nose. After settling for a few moments, he reflected on what the Winemaker had said: "Savor – combine the external with the internal." But what did that mean? He racked his mind, and was tempted to pull out his phone for a quick definition, but instead just meditated on the word 'Savor.'

Soy sauce is savory, so are mushrooms, he thought. Both are earthy and good, but so is sucking on a good piece of chocolate. That is savory also. Umami is also savory, which translates to good taste. He sat in focused silent meditation for a few more deep breaths and then pondered, Savor, having a good taste, something that is enjoyed.

So, the Winemaker told me that I am not savoring things. I see them, understand them, recognize them, but what? What am I missing? He could feel that he was close to some insight. It was right there, but he couldn't identify it. It started to create anxiety in him, and a Winemaker quote flashed in his mind: "Only trust direct experience." At that moment he understood. A faint distant light broke through the haze in his mind and he knew what he was missing. It was so simple, so obvious, but it had taken him his entire life to come to this point of time, sitting under a pine tree with needles poking him in the butt.

If I want to follow a true path, it must be a path of passion. It must be a path that makes me happy and to feel complete. And that thing is so obvious! I have to tell the Winemaker!

He jumped up excitedly and stumbled because his leg had fallen asleep. He briskly walked around the pond to his car. Moments later he was back at the winery. It was closed, and the Winemaker was gone.

CHAPTER 21

The next morning Joe was pumped full of energy. Mary and Lucy were still out of town, and today was the Winemaker's party. Joe finally had an answer to the Winemaker's question. He was excited and there was a spring in his step as he hopped out of bed at 5:00. A quick cup of tea, and then he hit the zafu for twenty minutes of mindful meditation. Sweet smells of lotus wafted in the air, where the incense burned next to the gold statue of a frog meditating. With a singling bowl between his knees, Joe felt a complete sense of calm.

Some days meditation is a breeze. The body relaxes into a silent, still state, muscles relaxed and the mind calm and tranquil. The sounds around you come, go and leave without disturbing the stillness of the mind. Other days, mediation can be a challenge: the body is fidgety, the mind darts to and fro, and the calming sense of deep breathing is elusive.

And then there is the enlightening meditation. The mind is focused and concentrated but active. A movie is playing in the mind's eye, the conscious brain watching the scenes unfold. There is an excitement, a bundle of energy that is waiting to burst forth. This is the moment that many athletes and people of extreme skill say is the entry point to 'the zone.'

The zone is where time stands still. The body and mind are in unison. The mind is empty, and the body knows; the body does and the mind watches as if in a dream. Joe was almost in the zone, just a few more steps until he reached the precipice. From there he would launch into a new path. He would become Joe 2.0.

His mind was calm as a possible future scrolled out in front of him. He was there, in the moment, looking forward as far as his mind's eye could see. This path felt right. It was wholesome and fulfilling, and it excited Joe. He had finally found the missing piece and was now ready to act.

He sat in the darkness sipping his second cup of tea. Holding the cup close to his lips, the rich aromas and steam filled his nose. It was cold outside, but a fire was building within him. He blew the steam off the cup and took a small sip, 'savoring' every moment, mentally preparing for his big reveal with the Winemaker. A small leather-bound journal sat next to the meditating frog statue. Joe slowly flipped through the pages, reading the brief statements of his Gratitude Journal.

Every morning after mediation he would jot down a few things for which he was thankful for and in areas he gave gratitude. He always tried to find the small event for which he was thankful that was unique from any other entry. He had been dutifully writing in his journal ever since his second destemming at the winery when Rachel had asked him a very interesting question.

Instead of the standard "How are you?" she had asked, "What are you thankful for?" Not being mindful, out of habit Joe blurted out, "Fine, and you?" Rachel gave him a look that pierced right through him. Joe realized his mistake, and then tried to fumble for an appropriate answer to her question, but came up blank.

Rachel could see the confusion in Joe and calmly and simply asked again, "What are you thankful for today Joe?" He fumbled and stuttered, but just couldn't come up with an answer. "Joe, how can you ever be happy if you don't appreciate or recognize the bounty and beauty that is always around you?" Joe looked up with questioning eyes. Rachel took him by the elbow and led him to a quiet table in the tasting room, where she looked deeply into his eyes. He felt as if she was looking deep into his soul, which was empty and without form. He felt ashamed and sad.

With a compassionate smile, she said, "Gratitude builds happiness. Being appreciative of what happens sets down a good foundation for living a happy, helpful life. Some people focus on what they don't have and are miserable. Some people focus on what they do have and are happy.

"Living a life of gratitude and happiness is a skill that is not often taught and must be learned, practiced and followed in all aspects of life.

"And this is a challenge in the hyper-media, hyper-advertising, hyper-drama, hyper-conflicted, hyper-aggressive world we live in today. We are constantly bombarded with what is wrong in the world, including wars, murders, rapes, disasters and social unrest. With today's technology, if an incident happens anywhere across the globe, it can immediately be on billions of people's news feeds, fed into their minds one drop of poison after another. Why does this happen? I have two guesses. One is money – people like to see gritty things, which therefore sell more advertising. Advertising is telling us why our lives suck because we don't have the gizmo that they are selling. So that is the first reason, money. The second reason is that in a morbid way, we all like to hear about someone less fortunate than ourselves so that no matter how much our lives suck, we can point to them and say, 'Glad it's not me.'

"But this path is filled with thorns, traps and mental disasters, and is a horrible way to view the world. It only leads to unwholesome desires, thoughts and actions. People on this path tend to be either self-pitiful or aggressive.

"The self-pitiful ones down deep like to feel bad and victimized, and constantly think they are being taken advantage of. They think that the universe is out to get them, and for some silly reason think that they are the cause, victim or result of some cosmic plot to get them.

"Now the second type are the aggressive ones. They are the pushy ones who always want to be treated first, the ones who walk with the air of entitlement. They deserve to be something that they are not, and will often complain about the lucky break someone else got and how they deserve the same privileges.

"Thousands of years ago, the Buddha developed a theory on why people suffer, which he named the 'Four Noble Truths.' The first noble truth is that life involves suffering. Even when things are good, there is a general anxiety about a darker future and the loss of good fortune. The second noble truth is that the cause of suffering is due to attachment and craving. If we want something and don't get it or lose it, then we suffer because we are attached to it. Once we have it, we don't want to lose it, which leads us to the third noble truth, and that is that there can be an end of suffering. By embodying the first two precepts and the full understanding of what causes suffering, we can remove suffering by changing our beliefs, attachments, and attitudes. The fourth noble truth is that there is a path with eight focuses that will help remove suffering. This is called the Eightfold Path.

"If you begin to focus on what is good and wholesome and stop doing things that are harmful and destructive, your life will get better for you and those around you. Now to do this, you must practice, and one of the simplest ways is to keep a Gratitude Journal where you record the positive things that happen in your life. On rough days, this book is an inspiration or a guide to keeping you on track. Wait a minute, I'll be right back."

Joe sat there trying to comprehend what Rachel had said.

She returned bearing a gift. She handed Joe a small leather-bound journal with a matching pen. "Here you go Joe: think good thoughts, do good things and be grateful for the abundance that surrounds you." She handed him the book with a smile. Then she turned and walked away leaving Joe holding this very thoughtful gift. From across the room, she yelled, "You're welcome."

###

Joe took up the gold pen and opened the leather-bound Gratitude Journal. He wrote, "I am thankful for meeting Rachel. I am thankful for meeting the Winemaker. I am thankful for finding my new direction in life." Then he sat back and reflected on the last few months, and on the strange, wonderful and curious path he had trod.

It started on a very crappy day when his life was in shambles. He was lost, scared, confused, and was in a place he didn't want to be. Now, months later, he was less lost, less confused and about to embark on a new chapter in his life, and he was excited. He thought back to a joke Jerry, who was part of the Crush Crew, loved to tell everyone. Jerry was the ringleader – "just one more press, just one more bucket, just one more ton" – forever the optimist, forever happy and upbeat. But he would joke, "Before enlightenment, chop wood and carry water. After enlightenment, chop wood and carry water." And after hearing this a hundred times, Joe finally understood: it is not what happens in life, it is what you make or do with it that matters. He smiled, closed his little journal and patted it affectionally. "'Til tomorrow good friend," he said, then set it down next to the meditating frog statue again. He finished his second cup of tea, took a shower, shaved and got ready for the Winemaker's end of season Crush Crew Party.

He had no idea what to expect - and knowing that he was taking Larry as a guest put his nerves on edge. He had worked for Larry for five years, but hardly even knew the man. They spoke infrequently, and Joe didn't know a single thing about him, apart from his being a 'jerk' and his incompetent boss. Why did I invite Larry? On this monumental day, I am bringing someone who I don't know, who nobody else knows, and who can be a total prick. Just then his phone rang. It was Larry.

"Hey buddy…"

Buddy?! Joe thought.

"Look, I know this is a huge favor, but my car got a flat tire and I need new brakes, and the only appointment is at 11:00 this morning. I don't have a way to get there and drop off the car, and I don't know anyone else, and I really need your help, and could you... help me fix my flat and then follow me over to the shop so that I can drop off the car and then take me to the party?"

Joe silently shook his head in disbelief. "Sure Larry, what's the address? I can be there in an hour," he said, thinking, Karma, remember karma.

It was just past 11:00 am when they got the car dropped off. Larry said, "Hey buddy, what do you want to do 'til the party?"

Joe had skipped breakfast to help Larry out and was on the famished side, so he suggested an early lunch at a burger and brewhouse that was close to the winery and not too far from the Winemaker's house. Joe thought it would be a great time to reflect and think about what he was going to tell the Winemaker, but it didn't turn out that way – not at all.

As soon as they sat down, Larry launched like a ballistic missile into a convoluted and depressing monologue about all the unique difficulties confronting him. It was as if Larry had never had a conversation with another adult. He blamed his mother for not bringing him up properly to deal with conflict and change. He blamed his father for not pushing him in sports so that he would be more integrated and able to socialize. He blamed his older brother for not supporting him when they were kids and always beating him up. He blamed his sister for laughing at him when he tried to date girls, putting his inability to form relationships down to this. He blamed the company for forcing him into a management position. He blamed his co-workers for not supporting him because they didn't understand him. He blamed politics for high taxes, the crumbling middle class, and homelessness.

Joe tried to stay on the high ground and listened patiently as they first sat down, as they ordered their beers, as they placed the orders, and as the food was delivered. Eventually, he was at a breaking point. Hold it together Joe. Be supportive. Don't lash out even though you want to. Stay calm, he repeated to himself.

Joe finished his burger, fries, and beer. He desperately wanted to flee the depressing vomit spewing from Larry, but he remained quiet and attentive while his mind raced. What would the Winemaker do? What would he say? He wouldn't put up with this dribble, would he? What should I say? What should I do? Then it struck him, and he knew what he must do.

He started gently, and then built a little more intensity, but not to the point of being confrontational. "Larry, it sounds like there is a lot of stuff tucked away in that head of yours. It sounds like your attic needs cleaning out – you know, to get rid of the dusty stuff. Tidy up the place, make it more presentable."

Larry just stared back at Joe, jaw hanging down between bites of his burger.

"Now you know, you put all that stuff up in your attic. You let it pile up to the point where the floor below is about to collapse. You choose what to put up there in your head and what you did not. Unfortunately, Larry, I hate to tell you this, but you have bad taste."

171

Larry remained befuddled, mouth hanging open in confusion.

"I think you need to throw away all of the bad stuff – the excuses and such – and take responsibility for what you decide to keep." Joe could see that his lightheartedness and analogies were not going over well at all. He was crashing and burning, and now he wasn't sure what to say, but he pressed on. He thought, Oh Grasshopper, you have much to learn still.

"Larry, I don't want to be a dick, but you have to take responsibility for your life. While it is easy to blame others, you will find that this will lead you into despair. You must own it, whatever you do. Sometimes it works and sometimes it doesn't, but at least you are steering the ship."

There was a long awkward silence as Larry finished his burger. Joe was beginning to think he had handled this whole thing badly when Larry looked up and said, "Joe, this is all your fault."

"What?! My fault. How can your life by my fault?"

There was a long strenuous pause, then Larry said, "Joe, I watched you from my office. I watched you change from a quiet, meek guy who didn't talk much or share much, even with your friends. And then, you realized that this merger was failing well before anyone else. You started talking to people. I heard you in the lunchroom talking about finding purpose and passion. I watched you help people move on in life. You inspired so many people and gave them the courage to follow their dreams, and to fulfill a legacy. And the more you helped, the more you grew and the more I began to feel jealous. I wanted to move on, I wanted all those things that you talked about, but I was stuck in a bath of self-pity and you didn't help me."

Joe was stunned.

"And every day you helped more and more people, but you ignored me. You would walk past my office, aloof and not caring about me. I began to resent you for this. You seemed to be moving on along with everyone else, leaving me behind. Loser Larry stuck on the sinking ship. That's what you called me, right Joe? You would call me Loser Larry.

"And now you are telling me to my face that I have bad taste and that I shouldn't blame others. Well, you know what Joe?" There was an awful, lengthy pause. "You're right."

Joe felt like he had been hit by a speeding bus.

"My mother died when I was only seventeen. My father was long gone, with one bimbo or another. When she died, I took over the house. I was a kid, I didn't know what I was doing and everyone kept taking advantage of me – so I started blaming them for my problems, never really growing up or moving on. In many ways, I am still that scared seventeen-year-old kid, old enough to know, but not old enough to do, to take responsibility. My mother used to talk to me the way you do. She was a stern woman who wouldn't take crap from anyone.

"When she died, I had nobody to take care of me, to nurture me or to call me out when I was doing bad, until now. Joe you are the first person in over twenty years to call me out – just like my mother would do. I guess I am Loser Larry. And even though you called me out, thanks."

"Look, Larry, every day we take thousands of little steps, but it is your choice on which steps you will take. You are responsible for your path and I am responsible for my path. If you want, we can work this out together. But for now, my friend, we have a party to attend."

173

Darius Miller

CHAPTER 22

The Winemaker lived in a quiet neighborhood just a few miles away from the winery. Joe could see that many of the Crush Crew students had already arrived, and they had to park some distance away. "Okay, Larry: please, please, please don't be a dick and start on the woe is me crap. These people will eat you alive and toss you out like a bad egg."

"Don't worry, Joe. I will show off my good side!"

"What good side?"

They both burst out laughing.

About twenty of the Crush Crew were already there, clustered in groups all around the house. Joe smiled and hugged everyone he passed by. Everyone was cheerful and had a drink in hand. Joe hadn't seen Larry since they walked in the door, which made him nervous. These were his people, and he desperately hoped Larry wouldn't make a scene, but he was missing.

Joe wandered through the house until he spied the koi pond in the back yard – the inspiration for the winery. Sixteen hungry faces mouthed 'feed me' at the surface. There was a small waterfall in the back babbling away. Joe sat on the edge of the pond and watched the fish trying to grab his attention when Kasha came up, "Hey Joe, enjoying the scenery?"

"So, this is where it all began? It all makes sense now: air, water, fire, and earth, all here," he said pointing, to the sky, pond, fire pit, and landscaping.

"But you're missing the best part, Grasshopper," she said jokingly. "The people. It's the people who come together that make the magic happen. And speaking of people, the Winemaker has called everyone to meet in the living room.

Let's go," she said wrapping her arm around his shoulder and dragging him along.

The living room wasn't that big, and with more than thirty people standing around, it was cozy. Joe spotted Larry across the room holding a drink and chatting with Bob who ran a tech company. Lisa was busy passing out bundles of presents for everyone – three neatly wrapped gifts all bundled together with a bow. The Winemaker stood in the arch facing everyone. "Thank you all for coming out today for this year's Crush Crew Party. I feel so humbled and blessed by each one of you. Your love, your kindness, and support are the most valued things in my life. Without you, Koi Zen Cellars would not be the place it is today. Years ago, Lisa and I wanted to create a place that was full of friends and good times; and thanks to you, that is what it has become.

"I wish to share with you a few small tokens of my appreciation. Please open the small rectangular box." Inside the box was a small, very sharp pocketknife. The crew looked around, some smiling and some confused. "Every day I carry a knife in my pocket and it makes me feel complete. When you have a knife readily available, you will be amazed at how many times it becomes useful. It is a tool that helps us live a slightly easier life. Think of it as a tool to help you cut through the problems in life, or the tangled messes that happen, or the bagel for breakfast. But please don't hurt yourself."

Everyone giggled.

"Now please open the small square box." Paper rustled and more smiles appeared. Each box contained a small pocket flashlight. "You all know that I also always carry a flashlight. It is easy to get lost when it is dark, and it is hard to find solutions to problems that face us in life without a little beacon of light. Carry it always and use it often.

"Now please open the larger gift. This book is all about wine: the types of wine, wine regions around the world, types of grapes and production. The world of wine is huge, and I hope this book will inspire you to continue to learn and to explore. Unlike a book, which has a beginning and an end, learning should never stop. I encourage you to always continue to learn, to prosper and to lead by example."

Everyone cheered and had begun to disperse when the Winemaker commanded their attention. "I have one more gift to give. I have a very special gift for a very special person who had brought me joy and has taught me a few things along the way. Where is Grasshopper?" Everyone looked around and then started pushing Joe forward towards the Winemaker.

Joe stood beside the Winemaker wondering if this was a joke, but the Winemaker was serious. "My friend Joe here came into the winery a few months ago smelling like crap – yes, I said crap, and he did, from head to toe. But he has transformed over the last few months. At least he took a shower." Everyone laughed. "I have watched Joe transform from a confused individual who lacked direction and had no purpose."

"Hey, wait a minute," Joe blurted out, "I had a purpose." At this, people laughed so hard they nearly cried.

"We know, Joe," the Winemaker replied, still chucking, "but now you have a real purpose in life. I can see it in your eyes. And I wanted to give this to you." Lisa was standing at the Winemaker's side holding a neatly folded black bundle, and she handed it to Joe. Joe tentatively took it and unfolded it. It was a black windbreaker. On the lapel was the Koi Zen Cellars logo, and embroidered below it was the words "Assistant Winemaker."

Joe cried tears of joy, and the sentiment spread through the Crush Crew like wildfire. He was humbled and, in that instant, knew that the Winemaker had already known what Joe's new direction would be, without ever saying a word.

Epilogue

The lights shone harshly into his eyes and the crowd was a sea of dark faces. A thousand people hung on every word, everyone sitting on the edge of their chairs waiting for the next words. "And in conclusion, we have learned that you must 'see' reality, you must 'swirl' your thoughts to look at life from all different viewpoints, you must 'smell' the things around you and get to know them, you must 'sip' and become one with the experience, not through a book or a movie, but by doing.

"And finally." The crowd was silent, not a breath was heard. "You must 'savor' life. You must drink it, consume it, become part of it, and enjoy it. Cheers."

The crowd went wild. Row after row people stood applauding the motivating speech. Joe bowed and walked off stage.

Mary grabbed him and gave him a giant hug. "Oh, Joe you are so wonderful. That speech really inspired those young minds. You seem to be able to resonate with these graduating students. I'm so proud of you. Oh, don't forget, you have a book signing later tonight, and Dr. Bill wants you to be a guest speaker on his TV show later next month."

###

Joe's transformation did not happen overnight – it took many years of hard work and long hours to achieve the ambitious goals he had set for himself. In the beginning, he was filled with doubt and considered giving up on many occasions, but in his heart, he knew that if he did give up, he would regret his decision forever. In the end, he influenced hundreds of thousands of people – not bad for an 'Average Joe.' But Joe was not average, he was unique, just like everyone and everything else in the universe; just like you and me.

Each day he would approach life with the eyes of a baby, constantly 'seeing' the world as if for the first time. He understood how his past experiences and prejudices would cloud reality, but by understanding this he was able to see through the mist and clouds that formed in his mind. Through this, he saw the abundance and beauty that surrounded him, no matter where he went or what he was doing. After years of practice, he could see myriad sides of a problem or an opportunity, giving him the freedom to choose how he would react and the path he would take.

No matter how clouded his world became, the lighthouse that guided his life shone bright and beckoned him towards it. He could see the path before him and could understand how to better navigate the obstacles that life threw at him. He still carried the flashlight in his pocket (he lost his knife at airport security – oops!)

He knew that he was on the right path, though he never became complacent and always trod with keen observation and attention. He became fascinated by the concept of choices. While some believe their lives are predestined by their genetics, race, education, upbringing, social status, job or whatever people identify with as 'me,' Joe felt different. He felt free and constantly 'swirled' his life as often as possible. He understood, to some degree, how the ripples he formed in the universe would resonate, and used that to stir things up by trying new approaches and tactics. With the ability to see his choices, and the confidence to swirl things around, he became wildly successful – not because he was lucky, but because he did the right thing at the right time in the right place, just as a grape grows best in a specific environment or terroir.

Much to Mary's, Lucy's and Jack's delight, Joe became an exceptional cook. The simple act of cooking inspired him to create, explore and expand his palate. He became accustomed to 'smelling' everything he came across. This raised a few eyebrows in the grocery store and the park, but through this simple act, he became an expert smeller. He could identify which spices were used in a dish and was able to replicate any dish he tasted, not through a recipe but through his memory, tastes, and senses. This ability fascinated and frustrated family and friends, because he could never describe how he cooked since it was all through smell and instinct; the concept of a measure or recipe was foreign to him.

In business relations, he could 'smell' opportunity and problems well before anyone else. His senses were highly attuned to his environment, and Mary often claimed he had ESP. He could almost predict the future through his keen observations and honed skills. Just as one can see seconds ahead while driving, he could see his life as it moved into the near future.

Joe 'Sipped' life constantly. No matter what he was doing, he was drinking the experience up. It didn't matter if it was 'good' or 'bad,' for he had long dismissed passing judgment on experience, knowing that you can always see things from a different viewpoint. He always wanted to try something new, something novel and something unique. He would travel to unique grocery stores that carried a product with labels he could not read and tried everything. This, combined with his culinary skills, unfortunately often created what some would call 'interesting dishes.' But using only smell and taste, he could fine-tune any dish into a masterpiece.

He 'savored' life to the fullest. He immersed himself in understanding, remembering and tweaking everything he did. Little was ever done without complete mindfulness and presence. After the transformation, he enjoyed life to the fullest, never living in the past or projecting his desire into the future. He lived in the moment, fully understanding where he was headed, why he was headed that way and fully cognizant of any opportunities or obstacles that may happen along his path.

His positive attitude was uplifting to those who surrounded him, not for being a panacea or fantasy, but because he was able to capture, appreciate and reflect the true qualities of the beauty of life. Hardly ever a bad word, a harsh criticism, jealous comment or gossip left his mouth or entered his mind. He focused solely on what was positive and helpful.

Every thought, action, and expression was always backed by the question, "Is this for the good, or not?" and he always chose only to follow the wholesome path.

Joe would blush when praised, and demur, saying that he only did what seemed good at that moment and that helping people achieve their greatness was in the best interest of the universe. He had no delusions of grandeur that he was going to change the entire universe. He just wanted to help make the life of everyone he touched "Just a little better, one sip at a time."

Made in the USA
San Bernardino, CA
24 June 2020

73996272R00109